Trudeau's Canada

Truth and Consequences

D1316125

trudeau's canada

TRUTH AND CONSEQUENCES

PHILIP C. BOM

Guardian Publishing Co. Ltd.
ST.CATHARINES, ONTARIO

Trudeau's Canada: Truth and Consequences

National Library of Canada ISBN 0-920376-00-2

Printed In Canada

Contents

Abbreviations:

FFC — Federalism and the French Canadians
AP — Approaches to Politics
CC — Conversation with Canadians
AS — The Asbestos Strike

Preface

Almost a decade has passed since Pierre Elliott Trudeau became Prime Minister. Even though the man of tomorrow may resign today, or win the next election, he has made a permanent impact on Canada. Few countries can claim such a gifted and talented leader. As a statesman, not as a private person, he is worthy of in-depth reporting and critical scholarship. This is an analysis of his political philosophy and his plans for Canada. From the perspective of a political scientist, it was an exciting educational experience.

The 1970 October crisis sparked our initial interest. At that time Trudeau was asked how far he would go, and replied to the effect: Just watch me. Instead of merely watching, we began a study of his writings and representative speeches which increased after the 1975 October crisis. The desire to write grew out of a belief that few authors had been able to present a comprehensive interpretation of Trudeau's philosophy and its concrete application to Canada.

It is a responsibility of scholars to encourage truth in politics, especially in the exercise of public authority. The interpretation may still be controversial, but, like Trudeau, we hope the reader and reviewer will deal with the substance of a book, and not side issues. (FFC, p.77) Hopefully, it will receive a more liberal reception than another study on a previous Liberal Prime Minister.

It is also a scholar's task to remind people of the moral responsibility of citizenship. Trudeau wants the public to be educated into a sense of involvement in participatory democracy. He wants the electorate to use their heads. (AS, p.51; FFC, pp.119-120) Therefore, this study is an exercise in public education, seeking to contribute to a deeper understanding of the essentials of Trudeau's social philosophy. The purpose will have been achieved if citizens become politically aware, read with more discernment, and participate in representative democracy.

My excellent wife, Anthoinette, found the subject so interesting that she joined in reading most of the material. Her critical comments and continued assistance throughout the project were invaluable.

Finally, the book is dedicated to our parents, who have been a source of inspiration and support in countless ways. Like other Canadians, they chose this country for its freedoms and democracy. We hope their descendants may continue to live and work in the Canada they, the people, have built.

Easter, 1977

"... a prime minister 'gives himself' to his country.... But it does not necessarily follow that such a gift is always to the advantage of the recipients: there are some gifts one would do well not to accept, as the Trojans learned to their cost some years ago!''
Trudeau, 1958

"Of course there is need for doctrinaires of a sort, or at any rate for theoreticians who will constantly expound what they think to be the nearest thing to 'pure socialism'... the dreamers of today frequently become the realists of tomorrow; and the educational value of painting utopias has repeatedly been established by the eventual realization of such goals through the democratic process.''
Trudeau, 1961

"I dream. I dream all the time. I've always dreamt of a society where each person should be able to fulfill himself to the extent of his capabilities as a human being, a society where inhibitions to equality would be eradicated.... I conceive of politics as a series of decisions to create this society.''
Trudeau, 1969

Chapter I
Introduction

The Right Honourable Pierre Elliott Trudeau has been in office as Prime Minister for almost a decade. Although he has been politically active for the past thirty years, little was known about the man and his vision until he suddenly arrived on the federal scene in the early sixties and successfully sought the Liberal leadership. In coming to power, he aroused a politics of great expectation.

Much was written about Trudeau shortly after he became Prime Minister, but few writers have seriously analyzed the political thought he expressed earlier. Although most writings enhance our understanding to a considerable degree, none has been able to present a coherent and comprehensive framework of the thoughts and policies of Trudeau. Many writers approach him in terms of their own prejudices. They do not take Trudeau's theories and actions seriously and within a unified context. If parts of the puzzle do not fit their preconceived notions, Trudeau is supposedly a confused man, a man who does not know or understand his own mind, a paradox in office; or it was just his thinking aloud, hoping to spark debate, a slip of the tongue at an unguarded moment. Such comments are an insult to the intelligence and political genius of the Prime Minister.

The difficulty is that many journalists and academicians

approach Trudeau's philosophy and politics from their own or the traditional liberal perspective. They assume common usage of meaning when Trudeau uses words like freedom and democracy, federalism and liberalism, without critically examining these concepts within his perspective. For instance, Trudeau attributed only practical value to the concept of majority rule, within a liberal democracy - it is merely a convention. (AP, p.88)   In addition, "freedom" apparently includes what he designates as collective freedom such as is experienced in Cuba under a dictatorship, and which may lead to personal freedom. (FFC, p.209)   Few writers on Trudeau have an extensive philosophical knowledge which could make possible a critical theoretical understanding of the unity of thought and action on the part of Trudeau.

Those who think he is a complete pragmatist fail to distinguish between pragmatism as a philosophy and being pragmatic in strategy and tactics ("what will work" in politics); and, consequently fail to read him correctly. "I am a pragmatist in politics, which does not mean that I do not have ideals," Trudeau told the Winnipeg Canadian Club in May 1968. Some "basic principles which I like to see applied in our country," such as federalism, constitutional reform, and human rights, must be understood in the light of the spirit of Trudeau's social philosophy. "But beyond these ideals, I am a pragmatist, I try to find the solution for the present situation, and I do not feel myself bound by any doctrine or any rigid approaches to any of these problems." He is not bound by any "doctrine" in strategy or rigidity in tactics, but, from his writings, he is apparently dogmatic in his basic principles which have much in common with democratic socialism.

Trudeau has "never been able to accept any discipline except that which I imposed upon myself." (FFC p.xxi) From his writings all indications point to the conclusion that the intellectual discipline he imposed upon himself was similar to that of international democratic socialism. (FFC. pp.124-130) Even when he joined the Liberal Party, he never publically renounced his socialism. In joining the Liberals, Trudeau turned his back not on socialism, but on the socialist party (NDP) which he had supported but never joined, because it exchanged "socialism for nationalism", preaching "national socialism". (FFC, p.xx) Trudeau is flexible in party and policy, but inflexible in discipline and principles. He is consistent in his social philosophy of "social radicalism" (AS, p.343), and pragmatic in strategy and tactics.

Consistency is one of the outstanding features of Trudeau's thought over several decades. Jean-Pierre Goyer, Minister of Supply and Services, told a Liberal Party caucus in the 1960's that he knows "Trudeau best by what he's written - and it's the best way to know him. He doesn't deviate from his writings. Just about everything he thinks is there." 1) During the fifties and sixties, Trudeau was an active supporter of radical social thought and actions, and the goals and policies of his Liberal government show a remarkable consistency with his earlier writings. From the 1949 Asbestos strike to the 1975 postal strike Trudeau has envisioned industrial democracy, with workers being paid in relation to their contribution to society. All this has become the framework for *The Way Ahead* (1976). In the 1950's he championed participatory democracy in the universities; in the 1970's he was actively promoting it both within the Liberal Party and in Canada as a replacement for representative parliamentary democracy. In 1964 he wrote about the powerless group preaching separatism for Quebec as a minority seeking to turn the pages of history back to tribalism, and in 1976 he repeated this concept after the Parti Quebecois victory. In 1967 Trudeau stated that any Canadian should have the right to use and learn either French or English, going well beyond what the BNA Act specified.(FFC, p.56) In the 1970's his Liberal government pushed through extensive bilingual programs under the mistaken assumption that this would save the union of Canada. In 1965 he suggested that English-Canadian nationalism might push Quebec towards separatism, and in 1976 again tried to place the blame for separatism at the feet of the English Canadians on several different occasions, one of which was during his October visit to Japan. On each issue which Trudeau considered important enough to warrant a written statement or article, he has remained committed and consistent to the same priorities and policies both before and after he became a member of the Liberal Party.

Since there is no indication that Trudeau has altered his view of society and basic principles which he seeks to apply in Canada, one can assume that he has remained socialist-oriented and has not accepted the traditional Liberal philosophy and perspective of society. However, within socialism there is a wide divergence of philosophy, ranging from social-gospel socialism to the totalitarian communist version. For example, there is a difference between NDP social democrats who believe in parliamentary democracy as an end and socialism as a means, and the more Marxist-Leninist democratic socialists who stand for socialism first and democracy as a means.

The Prime Minister wants to restructure fundamentally three hundred years of industrial relations, a hundred years of foreign and defence policy, fifty years of obsolete "superstructures" in Quebec, and thirty years of tinkering with a mixed free market system. He radically restructures a Liberal Party, Parliament, national policy and (in the planning stage) the Constitution.

The Prime Minister is a man with a single world vision to be advanced by means of multiple strategy and tactics. He may resort to double talk, but is not guilty of Orwellian "doublethink". He is consistent in his thought so that he does not have to change his views on China as a private citizen in 1960 and as a Prime Minister in 1968. Nor would he, according to his friend and fellow traveller to China, Jacques Hebert, "like to repudiate his writings of yesterday." (Prefatory Note, AP, p.22) His writings on violence, confrontation, liberty, dignity and democracy "are still shockingly relevant, as if nothing had happened in Quebec for twelve years." (AP, p.17)

Much has happened to Canada during the decade Trudeau has been in the federal government. His writings are still surprisingly, if not shockingly, relevant. Trudeau is a man with vision and decision, even if it takes him and his political descendants ten, twenty, or fifty years to build that Canada and world community which he seeks to construct. He has been consistent in his conception of the course of world history. In his introduction to one of Trudeau's books, John T.Saywell, one of Trudeau's early supporters for the Liberal leadership, wrote that "consistency is, in fact, the most remarkable quality of Mr.Trudeau's thoughts and actions over the past two decades." He added advisedly: "Trudeau is an experiment in Canadian public life.... The result will bear watching." (FFC, pp.vii,xiii) Such consistency can be more an evidence of dogmatic certainty than of open-mindedness and traditional pragmatic liberal politics.

For the purpose of this book, Trudeau's writings have been analyzed and it was assumed that he meant exactly what he wrote. The topics dealt with are issues which have (pre-) occupied him as a citizen, academician, and as Prime Minister. We have quoted extensively from his writings and speeches to be factual and fair in evaluating his thoughts and actions. Other than his own writings, there are few direct clues to outside influences on his intellectual discipline. Occasionally, when he feels insulted or misunderstood, such as the case when commentators continually referred to him as Galbraithian, he feels the need to correct them by saying that he has been more influenced by economists Joseph Schumpeter and Wassily Leontief. The writings of Lenin and Mao will occasionally be quoted to show parallels and similarities. This study is a critical analysis of the Prime Minister's public philosophy, not of his private mind.

There is an integral unity of direction in Trudeau's overall goals for Canada. One cannot separate policy concerns in one segment from those of another. It is probably the first time in Canadian history that there is so much emphasis at the planning level to make sure all policies are consistent with Trudeau's unity of direction. For instance, one cannot approve of his program in the economy and divorce it from what is happening to representative parliamentary democracy. From his radical perspective, he is restructuring the political, social, and economic institutions of Canadian society.

Trudeau has much intellectual integrity, but his political integrity has been found wanting. He has every right to be in politics, espousing his vision for Canada, whatever that may be. Although his consistency over three decades would seem to indicate that he is still a radical socialist, Trudeau is not a communist, let alone a member of a communist party. He has said "that communism has nothing to do with my approaches" (AP, p.62), and that he is not an agent of "the international communist conspiracy."2) At the time of Mao Tse-tung's death; the Prime Minister mentioned that he does not agree with Mao's Marxist philosophy. It would be contrary to his own discipline, if not an insult to his intellect, to rely authoritatively on Mao, Lenin, or even Marx. "The politicians who invoke the argument from authority demonstrate not only the weakness of their own intellects but their contempt for the intellects of their audience."(AP, pp.66-67) It would also be difficult, if not impossible, to impose the discipline of an authoritarian party on a political personality like Trudeau. He has not blindly applied Marxist principles or slavishly followed Maoist strategy and tactics, but has integrated and applied his radical and critical theory in an original and concrete manner to the historical circumstances (the French fact) and political situation (federalism and length of Liberal Party in power in Ottawa) in Canada. If he ever were to submit himself to the iron discipline imposed by an authoritarian party, he would, according to his own criteria, lack intellectual integrity. However, he has no moral right (human or political) to hide his radicalism behind a liberal philosophy, Party and Parliament; empty them of their traditional meaning, destroy their direction, and in the process deceive the people, misleading them to follow a leadership democracy.

It is Trudeau's radicalism, his commitment to internationalism, which has led to a politics of confrontation with Rene Levesque's national socialist Parti Quebecois in the 1960's and 1970's. Prophetically, these two protagonists are now in power. Looking back may help us understand what lies ahead.

Notes

1. Martin Sullivan, **Mandate '68**, p. 122.
2. Prefatory note to P.E. Trudeau and J. Hebert, **Two Innocents in Red China.**

"...the separatist counter-revolution is the work of a powerless petit-bourgeois minority [who]...want to make the whole tribe return to the wigwams by declaring its independence."
Trudeau, 1964

"Civil disobedience and the use of violence became the commonplace of the new confrontation politics."
A Foreign Policy for Canadians, 1970

"Life is confrontation...."
Trudeau, 1970

Chapter 2
Reflections on Quebec and confrontation

A political earthquake struck Quebec on November 15, 1976. The tremors were felt throughout Canada. The momentous event was not an accident of nature, but was largely the outgrowth of actions on the part of men like Rene Levesque and Pierre Trudeau who, by the force of their ideas and will, have come to power. The men of the disestablishment have become the new establishment. They displaced the liberal-conservative consensus of the 1950's with the politics of confrontation in the late 60's and 70's. The decade of the 60's was a battle for the minds of the voters; and the 70's and 80's will be a battle for the ballots. The electoral success of Trudeau and Levesque marked the end of the so-called "Quiet Revolution" in Quebec and Canada and initiated the building of a "new society".

Historical Reflections

To understand better the new foundation of Quebec and confederation, it may be worthwhile to dwell on Trudeau's reflections on Quebec as presented in the book, *The Asbestos Strike*. In his review of this book, Andre Laurendeau, former editor of *Le Devoir* wrote that Trudeau "provides us with a hundred pages that will be talked about for a long time to come."1) These pages are highly relevant for they help explain why so much has happened in Quebec and Canada during the past twenty years. The type of "social radicalism" to which Trudeau was committed helps explain why he has been unable to empathize with the national aspirations of the last three Quebec governments: Union Nationale, Liberals, and the Parti Quebecois.

Trudeau has viewed history as a movement from tribalism to nationalism, and finally to a co-operative international society. Devotees of nationalism in Quebec (which gave rise to separatism) "despite their good intentions and courage, were for all practical purposes trying to swim upstream against the course of progress." (FFC, p.168) To move against the "course of progress" is to be branded a "counter-revolutionary ".

Unlike the various nationalists who sought the development of Quebec from an ethnic, national perspective, Trudeau has been an internationalist from the beginning, envisioning the development of Quebec from a historical world perspective. He wrote in *The Asbestos Strike* with the conviction of a radical social scientist who had discovered the universal law of historical development. Trudeau did not reflect on Quebec from a "right" liberal perspective. He approached Quebec from a New Left perspective. This explains why Trudeau reflected on Quebec from a materialist conception of history. It is from a perspective of scientific socialism that he perceived the significance of the Asbestos strike.

Trudeau did not proclaim objectivity, but claimed to be scientific by starting from the facts. However, it was his materialist vision of history which viewed the material conditions as the "real forces" in Quebec history before the strike. He attempted to demonstrate that the elaborate "superstructures" of church and national state "were bourgeois fads". (FFC, p.xxxiii) In *Cite Libre*, March 1961, he wrote that it "is more urgent to assail the lethargy of our people, to rehabilitate democracy and to attack our clerico-bourgeois ideologies than to look for the guilty parties among the English."2)   Laurendeau could not make up his mind whether Trudeau wrote as an historian or a polemicist. "Are these pages history or polemics?" asked Laurendeau. It was a false contrast, because Trudeau was not an objective liberal historian, but a polemical, action-oriented social historian. According to Gerard Pelletier, Trudeau, as a critical social scientist, "while never falling into any kind of pamphleteering excess, occasionally writes with considerable passion, giving his reasoned analyses the rhythm and vehemence of polemic literature."(FFC, p.xvi)

Although his introduction to the study of the Asbestos strike was a sociological analysis, it served his ideological purpose. He wrote with the passion of an activist scholar, a participant observer. At the time of the strike, Trudeau sought to radicalize politically the trade unionist for social and economic upheaval in Quebec. As a radical scholar he presented facts and figures "not to please the lovers of statistics"(AS, p.1), but to indicate the need for radical change in society. He was not interested in "remote historical facts" or all the aspects of idealistic ideas and institutional developments in Quebec. "I must confess that I am only interested in the past as a means of acting upon the future...."(AS, p.330) "For the same reason, I will not shrink from emphasizing those aspects of nationalist thought which are a burden on the present, and harmful to free and honest action."(AS, p.8) Aspects of Catholic thought were dealt with in a similar fashion. "By isolating some aspects of this thought, we may show the reader just how little... people were prepared to accept, interpret, and influence realities in this highly industrialized province...." (AS,pp. 6-7) He was to show how the social thinking in Quebec at the time of the Asbestos strike was "so idealistic, so a priori, so divorced from reality, in sum so futile...."(AS, p.6)

"On reading his essay," wrote sociologist Ferand Dumont, "one can only conclude that the thinking that he analyzes is absurd."3) That is precisely the impression social critic Trudeau desired to create: make official, ideological thought look morally and intellectually futile, and ecclesiastical and economic structures historically obsolete. Not surprisingly, his severe criticism was somewhat unbalanced and unfair.

In his radical critique of the church, Trudeau stated that we "must distinguish clearly between Catholic social ethics as expounded by certain popes who have been particularly attentive to the upheavals of modern society and the social doctrine of the Church as it has been understood and applied in French Canada."(AS, p.13) It was an important distinction, but not completely fair to Quebec in comparison with, for example, the Church in Latin America. Furthermore, Trudeau did not maintain the clear distinction, giving the distinct impression that he threw out the baby with the bath. He obviously has not thrown all his critical powers in favour of a Christian democratic party and a non-denominational Christian labour movement based on the social ethics of *Rerum Novarum.* Rather than a champion of Christian democracy, he became a proponent of democratic socialism, helping to secularize the Catholic trade unions in Quebec.

Trudeau not only criticized the Church for the absolutism of its social doctrine, but also blamed its educational institutions for the backward social science. He was critical about the Jesuit Ecole sociale populair whose fathers taught the social sciences "as deductive tools, by means of which - starting from 'great principles' rather than from facts - a docile people might be led in the right direction. This institution must therefore assume a large share of the blame for the fact that, in contempt of reality, social thought in French Canada took a narrow nationalist path...." (AS,p.28) and children of the poor attended primary school "where their readers and their arithmetic problems extol the bourgeois virtues and illustrate the glories of the free enterprise system." (AS,pp. 36-37)

University education was not much better, according to Trudeau. At the University of Montreal, students and teachers were ignorant of "real sociology", that is, scientific sociology. "Our official thinkers, with amazing constancy, ignored all the social science of their own day."(AS, p.13) At Laval, the social science faculty "lacked realism...it did not pay enough attention to the problem of the political destiny of our people. In this field, the Laval school produced only vague and abstract notions and concentrated on attacking monolithic nationalism."(AS, p.41)

Trudeau was somewhat unfair in his comparison. On the one hand he criticized Catholic universities for still teaching from a (moral) philosophical approach. On the other hand he criticized the faculties of law for failing to teach from a philosophical (sociological) approach to law, such as at Harvard University and its Law School, which he was privileged to attend in the mid-forties. However, most American law schools, like those in Quebec, were preoccupied with teaching the techniques of the profession (case studies) rather than philosophy of law. The Catholic universities in Quebec were not out step with Catholic institutions in North America. Trudeau applauded Laval's Dean, Father George Henri Levesque, for accepting the "fact that science eliminates prejudice, and recognized that the teaching of Catholic social morality cannot dispense with intellectual integrity." (AS, p.40) But how much intellectual integrity can a Catholic (institution) have if he (it) teaches from positivist principles of secular, scientific humanism? The positivist perspective in social science is no more "neutral" than the "great principles" approach. It, too, starts from great principles, such as the preconceived idea of inevitable progress and historical materialism. Rather than lamenting the disappearance of the "great principles" approach, Trudeau welcomed the liberation of the social sciences from moral philosophy.

Trudeau did not approach the political and industrial problem in Quebec in a "spirit of strictly scientific objectivity". He said that he was not interested in all aspects or facts of Quebec history, but mainly in the negative, nationalist aspect of the past in order to promote political, social, and academic upheaval in Quebec. His criticism of social science at Montreal was that it "did nothing to prepare people for the social upheaval in Quebec. At the most, it helped to prolong the hostility to change cultivated by the nationalist school system and by the professors of our social doctrine of the Church."(AS, p.39) These universities and faculties did not "train an elite capable of redesigning our social structures in the light of contemporary realities."(AS, p.37)

Trudeau was an early champion of the politicalization of the social sciences, faculty, and students on the campus for the liberation of the "city" - *Cite Libre*. Unlike the liberal and Catholic faculty at Laval, Trudeau was not blind to the "political destiny" of the people. He intended to produce practical ideas (class consciousness) and concrete action (agitation at the Asbestos strike and a call for a student strike), and concentrate on promoting social radicalism (*The Asbestos Strike*) and a "real" understanding of "monolithic" communism as he and Jacques Hebert attempted to do in their book on Red China. Trudeau was particularly critical of the Church's condemnation of communism and socialism (e.g., C.C.F.) and the Quebec government's nationalist criticism of international trade unionism. (cf AS, pp. 16,23,32,47,48) The Communist Party and the C.C.F. "were, as always, forbidden by the theologians of nationalism and the politicians of clericalism."(AS,p.52)

His radical commitment to internationalism helps explain his criticism of nationalism and conservatism of the National Union Party in Quebec. For instance, in reviewing the articles in *L'Action francaise*, a publication of the Ligue des droits de francais, Trudeau noted: "In going over all these writings, one cannot help thinking that nationalism blinds people to the real forces which direct the economy of a country. The common good would undoubtedly have been better served if our researchers had studied the unequal distribution of our provincial wealth less from the ethnic point of view and more from the point of view of social classes and the inequities inherent in economic liberalism. To do so, however, they would have had to attack the economic dictatorship with more vigour and devote to real reforms of structure (teaching, nationalization, planned economy, etc.)''....(AS,pp.31-32)

Trudeau holds out no hope that either the National Union or Liberal Party will enlighten the people of Quebec. ''Throughout this period, there was so little reason involved in our political discussions, at election time or in Parliament, that our politicians did not have to bother with the education of the Quebec voter. Elections were decided, now by the emotions of nationalism, now by the blandishment of 'white whisky'. In our political arenas, the passions dominated the scene, and the most unspeakable of them affected the governing process.(AS,p.50)'' The people were perpetually misled by the promises and passions of the politicians, because ''the French Canadians never use their heads when it comes to politics.''(AS,p.51) ''The Liberal Party has been miserably remiss in its simple political duty. Instead of educating the French-speaking electorate to believe in democracy, the Liberals seemed content to cultivate the ignorance and prejudice of that electorate.''(FFC,p.119) However, a national or liberal state, said Trudeau, ''cannot govern without considering the real relations of forces in the country.''(AS, p.56) The ideological forces of conservative nationalism or liberalism cannot stop the progressive forces of industrialization, in particular the industrial, international trade unions. ''The ideological forces have done little but divert or slow down these developments.'' (AS,pp.56)

In spite of all the opposition, including that of the Catholic labour movement and leaders, the secular Quebec labour movement ''forged ahead with implacable determination, impelled by internal forces and a logic which ignored whatever was not dictated by its own nature. Our peculiar ideologies certainly had the capacity to slow the progress of the movement, dam up its forces, and disparage its logic, especially in the early stages. Ultimately, though, it seems that the fortunes of the trade union movement, in Quebec as elsewhere, were largely determined by the degree of industrialization, the attitude of capitalism, and the political climate.'' (AS, pp.60-61)

The transition from the past to the future, according to Trudeau, can only be made by ''means of social radicalism.''(AS, p.343) Social radicalism, not ideologies of clericalism, conservatism, liberalism, and nationalism, is the road to industrial progress and institutional peace. Social justice, based on the findings of scientific socialism, will bring about an equal distribution of wealth for the people. ''Under the present regime, the remuneration of the worker is probably less than the surplus value of his productivity retained by his employers, and his contribution to society."(AS, p.66) Even if the present distribution of incomes is fair, it is not equal, especially in relation to the proletariat's contribution to surplus value and society.

If industrialization develops according to its "internal forces" and capitalism according to its inner logic, why cannot the workers, busy with making a living, await the inevitable withering away of the capitalist stage of industrialization? And, if it is true that "the list of demands of any labour union," according to Trudeau, "has done more to influence the destinies of our changing society than all the libraries filled by our official social thinkers" (AS, p.62), what is the role of an action-oriented intellectual? 4) What Trudeau was doing during the Asbestos strike may best be explained by one of his teachers, Joseph Schumpeter. According to Schumpeter, "... the role of the intellectual group consists primarily in stimulating, energizing, verbalizing and organizing this material (hostility toward capitalism).... Labor never craved intellectual leadership but intellectuals invaded labor politics. They had an important contribution to make: they verbalized the movement, supplied theories and slogans for it - class war is an excellent example - made it conscious of itself and in doing so changed its meaning. In solving this task from their own standpoint, they naturally radicalized it, eventually imparting a revolutionary bias to the most bourgeois trade-union practices...."5)

As an intellectual, Trudeau applied his critical method of scientific socialism to an education of the ordinary workers concerning the political theory of the "class struggle". Higher wages are not sufficient. He taught them that the present problem in Quebec was neither an ethnic nor racist question, but an extra-ordinary situation and circumstance which demanded a radical political answer. Without a radical theory there can be no radical socialist party. He believed that "the seed of radicalism can slowly spread" through the use of federalism. (FFC, p.127)

The danger was that the workers would demand higher wages and a shorter work week within a capitalist or mixed welfare system. The workers must learn to give priority to political demands. Trudeau feared that Quebec workers, like Quebec voters, did not use their heads. They worked with their hands, preoccupied with making a living, and accepted the hand-outs of the bourgeoise. Trudeau believed he knew what was best for their common good. "Their life is lived on the level of immediate experience. The imperious necessity of earning a living, of meeting their present needs, obliges them to rediscover practical possibilities by the constant application of the empirical method." (AS,p.65)

Trudeau was afraid that short-run successes (recognition, increased prestige, and pay hikes) would spoil the proletariat. He wanted to teach the trade unionists long-run lessons of the significance of the strike, lessons which were not so self-evident. The danger, according to Trudeau, of "pure trade unionism" mentality was that the strike itself could secure equality. "It is wrong to think that the unions are in themselves able to secure this equality." (AS, p.336) There was an even greater danger that the workers, even union militants, would feel the necessity to "assert the equality of working people within a conventional social framework".(AS,p. 341) The greatest failure, from the socialists' point of view, would be that the workers solved their problems within the capitalist system. Some "speak of a period of consolidation, of a modus vivendi with the political and financial powers based on mutual respect and understanding...." Trudeau's response to this pause in the radicalization of the unions follows."What sort of rubbish is this! After fifty years of servile and stupefied silence, have the mass of industrial workers but recently acquired the right to speak, only to hold their tongues with greater eloquence? At the very moment when Quebec society feels that it may catch up after generations of backwardness, are the gains of recent progress to be converted into a sterile conservatism, or into the traditional 'je me souviens'? It is a matter of urgent necessity that we reject these counsels of quietude."(AS,p.345)

Trudeau believed that his "theoretical considerations enable us to get a better grasp of the manner and extent of the change effected by the Asbestos strike in introducing a new measure of equality and justice into industrial relations." (AS, p.338) He grasped the necessity for a political consciousness of the proletariate, a political involvement of the workers on the basis of a new perception and "the most dynamic elements of this (C.L.C. labour) movement came to advocate that the progressive political forces be brought together in the bosom of a new left." (AS,p.343)

Trudeau did not have a democratic nationalist movement in mind, but a "social radicalism", and he hoped that the more enlightened nationalists of Le Devoir and L'action nationale "will one day come to realize that they will only be able to make the transition from the past to the future by means of social radicalism." (AS, p.343) He wanted to introduce radical equality in the name of social justice, and within a transformed political and economic system. In this system there would be complete equality of status for capitalists and workers, an equal distribution of the wealth of a nation, its natural resources and the fruits of progress. (AS, pp.336, 338, 339) There would also be participatory democracy in industry. In the new stage of industrial development, Trudeau said the workers themselves, not the businessmen, would determine their place in economic decision-making. The new industrial revolution would alter the basis and possessor of property and authority. (AS,p.348) Truly, it was going to be an industrial democracy with a real political democracy, where the majority of the people (not a minority of politicians) would participate in the decisions regarding the society of the future. (AS,p.348)

The Asbestos strike experience moved Trudeau to envision that "a new and contemporary power asserted its control over our destinies, the demons that bedevilled the course of history in our province were exorcised, the spell cast on our present by our past was broken, and a host of creative powers were unleashed in all fields." (AS,p.339) That was the significance of the Asbestos strike, not only for the Quebec province, but for the entire country. Trudeau conceived what not even the proletariat perceived, namely: "The Asbestos strike, however, was significant because it occurred at a time when we were witnessing the passing of a world, precisely at a moment when our social framework — the worm-eaten remnants of a bygone age — were ready to come apart. It is the date, rather than the place or particular industry, that is decisive. As it happened, it was the asbestos that caught fire! This book is dedicated to the history of that conflagration."(AS,p.67)

In 1948-49 Trudeau witnessed the fall of nationalist China. "It was necessary for him," writes Jacques Hebert, "to verify in the field the ideas he had acquired, to compare actual life with his teachers' theories about man and society. In other words, he had to go around the world." (AS, p.21) He returned just in time to bear witness to the fall of Union Nationale government in Quebec. "I fought their regime until its downfall in 1960." (FFC,p.xix) In Trudeau's initial *Cite Libre* article, he wanted to acknowledge the empirical existence of the French and Christian reality on the North American continent. All political concepts and traditions of past generations are to be systematically placed under doubt. It is not enough to survive or conserve. By means of functional social science, past values are to be swept out of the way as he prepared to construct a new man. All myths, beliefs, structures, and norms are to be tossed aside as obsolete and merely obstacles on the road to the new society. He wanted leaders to be radically rational. 6) Clearly this was not the writing of a coldly intelligent, liberal social scientist. It was not the language of a liberal labour lawyer, but that of an intellectual mind which had absorbed much Marxist-Leninist theory. A political radical who had rejected the "counsels of quietude" may be more democratic than violent, but the goal is the total overthrow of the bourgeois-nationalist regime and an entirely new system of institutions and values in Quebec and, later, throughout Canada.

   To accomplish his goal nationwide, Trudeau shifted his base and place of operation. The tactic of "reform" and the strategy of parliamentary democracy as a means appeared more useful as he joined the councils of quietude in Ottawa. As Prime Minister, more pragmatic and administrative means are available to help Canada face the "new economic era". Polemicist Trudeau's 1949-1956 radical thoughts on a real solution to the cyclical and inequitable problems inherent in economic liberalism — planned economy and industrial democracy — are now, decades later being applied by Prime Minister Trudeau. The government position in The Way Ahead (1976) maintains Trudeau's absolute commitment to industrial democracy and equal distribution of wealth to the workers.

The Politics of Confrontation

   The "drama at Asbestos was a violent announcement that a new era had begun." (AS,p.329) Since the 1949 conflagration, sporadic violence has punctuated the "new era" of politics.

   As a pamphleteer and Prime Minister, Trudeau has been consistent in his practice of the politics of confrontation for the purpose of social radicalism. "Life is confrontation...." (CC, p.87) Confrontation can take a democratic form of demonstration, civil disobedience, sit-ins, or protest marches, and it can take the form of violence: bombings and kidnappings. Trudeau has given priority to democratic means of confrontation and has taken a strong position against anarchists who primarily rely on violence to change society. In the sixties and seventies "when the younger generation believes that it has invented confrontation" it might be useful, according to Jacques Hebert, "to draw to the attention of those who, in their agitation, have not yet altogether rejected reflection" to Trudeau's reflections on man, violence, democracy, and the art of confrontation. (Prefatory note, AP. pp.21-22)

Personally, Trudeau dislikes violence. (AP, p.34) Does that mean he has professionally and philosophically rejected it outright? No. "In my political philosophy, I think that there sometimes is room for violence," he said in September 1971. "In my religion I really cannot think of cases where violence is justified." (CC, p.67)

The merit of democracy is that it "allows changes without revolution, without illegality. As long as we have freedom of speech and free elections , I think it childish and irresponsible to want to drag us out of our political ills by violence." (AP, p.56) He has maintained the "radical intellectual dignity" to renounce violence within a democratic system, but he does not renounce violence absolutely. "It repels me" (AP, p.52), but politically it may have to be preached or practiced. That is why he also has accepted a theory for its use under certain historical circumstances. "It's the circumstances which one also has to have a philosophy about." (CC,p.68) He has never rejected it out of principle. It depends upon his theoretical analysis of the circumstances and whether democratic means are available to achieve radical reform. "As a politician I've never had to face that because I've always lived in a democratic society." (CC, p.68) However, if so, why then did Trudeau in his first speech to the Asbestos strikers in 1949 so agitate the workers that labour leader Jean Marchand had to spend quite some time to defuse their desire for violence and restore calm and rationality. Although Trudeau stayed around for weeks, Marchand never invited him to speak to the strikers again. It appeared that Trudeau used the available democracy to stage confrontations within labour and academic circles — to the extent that there were some violent overtones in later actions. In October 1957, Trudeau launched the idea of a student strike at the convention of the National Federation of Canadian University Students (AP,p.83),an idea of confrontation which came to fruition in the new era of education in the late sixties and seventies.

From Trudeau's actions and writings, there is little indication that he viewed Quebec as a workable democratic society. Certainly, Quebec was not a pure democracy, but the democratic means of free speech and elections were available. Yet Trudeau used free speech to preach a gospel of revolt, "overthrow the regime", the old order. He had the "radical intellectual dignity" to agitate the workers to desire violence and students to boycott classes. By imparting a revolutionary bias, Trudeau theoretically guided trade unions and student organizations into a posture of confrontation and politicalization.

Confrontation has been an integral part of Trudeau's politics, past and present. In the early sixties, he called the national socialists in Quebec political reactionaries and the more militant ones counter-revolutionaries. Trudeau knew Rene Levesque in those days and both participated in informal discussions and the liberation of Quebec and the restructuring of society. The liberal Levesque served at one time as Minister of Natural Resources in the Liberal government of Premier Jean Lesage. As a progressive Liberal, Levesque nationalized Quebec's hydro companies. Trudeau dismissed this move by writing that the right nationalizes, the left socializes.(FFC,p.169)

As a nationalist, Levesque sought national independence "as broad and autonomous as the federal system can stand." He sought participation in a "true confederacy."7) In a confrontation in September 1967 in Quebec city, Trudeau strongly opposed special status for Quebec and proposed complete integration of the two languages and cultures which forced Levesque to take his own stand. Behind the scenes manipulation by Trudeau associates may have forced Levesque out of a leadership position within the Liberal Party. According to Martin Sullivan, Levesque's decision "was another development that may have been encouraged or even manipulated by the federal strategists." 8) Trudeau's confrontation pushed Levesque not only out of the Quebec Liberal Party, but the Parti Quebecois government toward a position of complete independence.

Another area in which Trudeau created a confrontation with Quebec was his success in persuading the Pearson Cabinet to drop its position of special status for Quebec. This was a remarkable success when one remembers that only Marchand supported Trudeau, who was Justice Minister, against the position of special status within the confederation. Former Justice Minister, Guy Favreau, and Quebec leader of the Federal Party, warned the Cabinet against Trudeau's dogmatic insistance "because he feared it might result in the breaking up of Canada. Trudeau feared Canada would break up by default if the challenge were not made."9) By reversing the

Liberal Party's position on Quebec, the possibility for a liberal-conservative consensus and politics of compromise was cut off.

In addition, Trudeau's strategists believed that there should be a dramatic confrontation at the Constitutional Conference in February of 1968. It was known that Pearson was stepping down and the various factions were promoting their man for the leadership. The confrontation would pit Trudeau against the nationalist Premier Daniel Johnson on nation-wide television. This encounter would build up the image of Trudeau as a potential Prime Minister, in particular among English Canadians, a man who alone could lead the country to greater unity. Many participants, including Prime Minister Pearson, were shocked at the aggressiveness of Trudeau's attack on Johnson.

Another confrontation, well covered by the media, took place the evening before the 1968 election which enhanced Trudeau's image and chances of winning. It was St. Jean Baptiste Day and the authorities expected unrest and demonstrations. Even though there was a strong potential for trouble and violence, Trudeau came because "I was curious. I wanted to see what was happening." and confronted the rioters. "I'm not leaving. I must stay." He stayed — violence intensified — and his national image as a cool leader in the midst of crisis was enhanced. After the election, Dalton Camp commented: "The separatists made a supreme contribution to the achievement of our majority Government. When you are lucky in politics, even your enemies oblige you." He thought a Liberal organizer who guessed the riot was worth 40,000 Liberal votes in Toronto alone "may have been guilty of understatement." 10) Rene Levesque's Movement Souverainete Association condemned all forms of violence and broke off meetings with radical Rassemblement pour l'independence (RIN). Later, the St. Jean Baptist Society released a statement: "All evidence indicated that the presence of the Prime Minister of Canada on the platform of honour was alone responsible for provoking the anger of the demonstrators." 11) It ruled out federal political presence from then on and the Society began to support the separatist movement. The RIN under Pierrre Bourgault had supported Trudeau for the Liberal leadership because Trudeau would "bring about separatism quicker than anybody else." 12)

If the July 1968 riot boosted Trudeau into an electoral victory, the 1970 October Crisis created a rationale for the assumption of extra-parliamentary powers. The kidnapping of a British diplomat and the killing of Pierre Laporte were perceived by the Prime Minister as much a threat to his government as to the Quebec government. It is revealing that he branded the FLQ members as "anarchists", as "self-styled revolutionaries". "They are not revolutionaries, for they propose no new structures of government." (CC, p.64) On national television, October 16, 1970, Trudeau described them as "misguided or misinformed zealots" who "resort to acts of violence in the belief that only in this fashion could they accomplish change." They are terrorists, he told the Liberal Policy Conference the following month, because they cannot "adapt to the patient workings of the democratic process...."

In his practical response to the "anarchists", Trudeau is consistent with Lenin. Lenin also took issue with anarchists who, in his opinion, were without clear political objectives. Lenin neither rejected violence on principle nor accepted it as the principal method of struggle. "Marxism rejects all abstract thinking and doctrinaire prescriptions about types of struggle. It calls for a careful study of the mass struggle which actually is taking place."13) Lenin also had a philosophy of the historical circumstances in which violence can be used, under certain conditions. It may be that under circumstances such as the availability of parliamentary means to overcome the class struggle, a violent "method of fighting is inopportune and inexpedient...."14) He warned against the harmful illusions of what terror can accomplish in a democracy. According to Lenin, the means may be parliamentarianism today and armed rebellion tomorrow. Trudeau believed that "so long as socialism is to seek fulfilment through parliamentary democracy" (FFC, p.128), he considered the use of violence as counter-productive. Violence diverts attention and energies from his strategy of achieving major transformations of man and society through parliament.

Trudeau did not panic during the 1970 October Crisis. He carefully planned his confrontation. His strong measures (invoking the War Measures Act) were uncompromising, meeting force with counterforce. There were academics and journalists who were very critical of Trudeau's extreme measures. Scholars still look for convincing clues as to why he acted in such a deliberate and decisive manner. Perhaps Lenin provides a clue. "Criticism — the keenest, most ruthless and uncompromising criticism — must be directed against those leaders who are unable — and still more against those who are unwilling — to utilize parliamentary elections...."15)

The Prime Minister acted on principle rather than out of "personal rancor" as John Gellner suggested. In his evaluation of the October Crisis, he concluded: "...the invoking of the War Measures Act cannot be called anything else but an act of political folly. The point is that if extraordinary powers can be assumed by government on as flimsy evidence of national danger as there was in October 1970, the same can happen again and again. The imposition of the Act has helped to polarize and to radicalize Quebec politics."16)Rather than an act of folly, it was an act of genius in the art of confrontation politics! Trudeau achieved both goals: the radicalization of Quebec, something for which he had always worked, discrediting the "anarchists", if not the moderate separatists in the process; and achieved extraordinary parliamentary powers as a precedent, coming through it all as the defender of democracy and national unity.

The image of Trudeau as a national unifier was weakened somewhat with the election victory of the Parti Quebecois in November 1976. Trudeau again used the art of confrontation in Quebec City early in March of 1976. He threatened to patriate the constitution unilaterally. On March 5th, he berated Premier Bourassa and called the Bill 22 language legislation "politically stupid", heaping coals on the fire of personal hostility toward the beleaguered Bourassa, which, not surprisingly, boiled over in the campaign. Quebec Liberal Finance Minister Ramond Garneau called Trudeau's speech " unjustifiably violent and arrogant ".17) Trudeau persistently refused to help Quebec pay the debt of the international Olympics, which created a climate of economic hardship. As elsewhere in the country, the disenchantment with the Prime Minister rubbed off on Liberal Premier Bourassa and fellow provincial Liberals. Trudeau's March remarks contributed to the anti-Liberal, anti-Bourassa attitude in Quebec. Finally, Trudeau's dogmatic insistence that separatism was a return to tribalism and that the only solution was to integrate fully the two cultures, demonstrated his inability to understand the national aspirations of many Quebeckers. Indirectly, the Prime Minister's hard-line contributed to the Liberal defeat and the PQ victory.

During the last weekend in January 1977 Canadians witnessed a sense of the rising expectations of confrontation. Again the Prime Minister went to Quebec City to practice the art of confrontation. He called Premier Levesque a "missionary of illusion" daring him to consider the up-coming by-elections as a mini-referendum on separatism. Levesque realized that the elections cannot be a referendum and called Trudeau an ostrich, a "defender of the status quo" who is "playing with fire" in Quebec. He said that Trudeau is using the same tactic as in 1968, appearing as the "great saviour, the historical saviour" of an "obsolete federalism" in an attempt to restore the momentum of Trudeaumania of the last decade. Trudeau delivered his main address before the Quebec Chamber of Commerce. Speaking without notes, he repeated what he wrote in *Federalism and the French Canadians*, and has been repeating ever since he entered federal politics in 1965. It was well received by the businessmen. The audience was swept off their feet and spontaneously sang "O Canada" in French. The strategy appeared to work again: Trudeau triumphed as the saviour of Canada.

The Quebec election of the PQ's may have weakened Trudeau's image as unifier, but not necessarily his leadership image. Just prior to the election, Roger Lemelin, publisher of *La Presse*, addressed Laval University's alumni association, saying that the Quiet Revolution has brought about a "sick society" in Quebec. "The first objective after 1960 was to get rid of the past, of the influence of priests, of teaching brothers, and the traditional school texts. New powers were put in place and the high priests of the old culture were dislodged."18) Already in the fifties, it was Trudeau's first objective to radically criticize schools and universities like Laval, agitating for radicalization of the social sciences, organizing student strikes, and promoting participatory democracy in universities. Ironically, Lemelin spoke at a time when Laval had been closed since September due to demands for participatory democracy. The radicalization of Laval will mean the end of the 125-year-old institution as an excellent Catholic and liberal university. But publisher Lemelin is consistent. He was an early supporter of Trudeau for the Liberal leadership.19) Railing against the marxists and maoists who disseminate their " stupid radicalism" through the secular schools and Radio-Canada, Lemelin again called upon Trudeau to step in to correct the sick situation. It seems rather strange to call in the person who carries much responsibility for uprooting traditional Quebec society with its pervasive Catholic influence — thus creating fertile soil for "stupid radicalism". It may be an irresistable invitation for Trudeau to step in with a clever strategy of radicalism through federalism.

The new situation in Quebec with the PQ in power, provided the Prime Minister with an opportunity to use the art of "politics of crisis" to replenish his leadership democracy. Soon after the Quebec election, he played up the strategy of crisis. "The crisis is real; the crisis is now, and the challenge is immediate." And in a moment of near panic, *The Toronto Star* editorialized on its front page that "Canada is in mortal danger, facing the gravest crisis since its formation in 1867." The editorial called for a "radical new deal" and a non-partisan government "to see us through this national emergency".20) Former *Toronto Star* editor Peter C. Newman also called for a non-partisan extra-parliamentary movement to preserve confederation, if necesary in a radically new form.21) *The Toronto Star* was critical of the Prime Minister's rigid federalism, but Trudeau has certainly met the editor's leadership requirement: "to awaken to our country's peril and banish the delusion that old attitudes, old policies and obsolete constitutional arrangements will see us through this national emergency." In actual fact, Trudeau has always been flexible on "federalism", but it has been his rigid radicalism, his internationalism, which has been a stumbling block for the national aspirations of conservative, liberal, and socialist Quebeckers.

With the above calls for a non-partisan leadership, Canadians are sleepwalking into a disaster with extra-parliamentary leadership. The Prime Minister may oblige with a "You asked for it" type of leadership democracy as he did with the wage and price control legislation. Immediately after the Prime Minister's address to the nation (November 1976), Manitoba Premier Ed Schreyer said: "I don't know that anyone here thinks there is anyone else who can do any better." Not surprisingly, there have been overtures between the Prime Minister and Schreyer, who supports the Anti-Inflation program. Not only would an alliance replenish Trudeau's leadership, but possibly replenish the depleted Liberal Party with social democrats like Schreyer. Rather than calling for an extra-parliamentary or non-partisan leadership, Canada should be calling for more power back to Parliament so that the people's representatives can implement their solutions.

The danger is not first of all to the electoral fortunes of a political party, but the future of freedom and liberal democracy in Canada. The danger is that people will be increasingly frustrated and confused, willing to vote for anyone who creates an image of strong leadership, thinking only about "saving " Canada without knowing what this new Canada will look like. In Quebec, voters who had been frustrated with the Liberal government's Bill 22, making French the official language in the schools, voted for Levesque, for one reason or another, who is determined to move even further on the French language issue. By early 1977, Canadians had some second thoughts about Trudeau as the unifier of Canada. He knows the people are not satisfied with his leadership, but, according to Hugh MacLennan, "this does not disturb" Trudeau. The Prime Minister understands "profoundly how to hold and manipulate political power."22) If so, this should disturb the public, especially now that Trudeau is the only strong man left in the Cabinet.

The Prime Minister's exercise in "crisis politics" is a consequence of his politics of confrontation . In the light of this principle, a possible pattern of politics presents itself. His confrontation in Quebec of September 1967 helped move Levesque outside the Quebec Liberal Party. Trudeau's confrontation in Quebec of March 1976 was partly responsible for the defeat of the Liberal Bourassa government. It put the social democrats of the PQ party in power. The selection of Trudeau as the new Liberal leader "signified the end of any possibility that Quebec might achieve special status", according to Jacques-Yvan Morin, Vice Premier and Minister of Education in the PQ government. 23) Trudeau's 1968 national electoral victory meant the end of liberal-conservative consensus for some kind of special status for Quebec. The politics of compromise had ended, the politics of confrontation became the new norm in Canadian politics, a nation-wide phenomenon. Trudeau's confrontation with demonstrators during the 1968 Montreal riots and with the FLQ in the 1970 October Crisis, confirmed on him the charisma of saviour of his country, especially among English-Canadians. More important, each of the above confrontations gave a boost to the radical movement within Quebec.

Now that Quebec is radicalized, Trudeau will turn more to the West and engage in a confrontation with the western provinces, in particular Alberta with its wealth of resources. 24) Speaking before the Canadian Club in Toronto (January 4, 1977) Saskatchewan's Premier Blakeney warned that the move Trudeau's government made in siding with the resource companies in their legal battle against the province is unique in the history of Canadian federalism.

After a decade of confrontation, both Trudeau and Levesque are in power. Rather than emphasize personal(ity) clashes between Trudeau and Levesque, Canadians should concentrate on the goals for which both the Prime Minister and Levesque are fighting. They conduct our political affairs of state from different stations, on separate tracks, but both hope to move Quebec and Canada in a similar, socialist direction. They differ on their political base (province versus country) and space (nationalism versus internationalism), but both stand for socialism and independence, liberation from a liberal capitalist continentalism. As the Prime Minister stated in his recent November address, he and Premier Levesque "disagree profoundly on the means." The difference is profound, but it should not blind people to the fundamental reconstruction of Canada. As the Prime Minister added, the basic question is not federalism, but what kind of new society Quebec and Canada will develop. It may be best to ignore   smoke-screens of verbal accusations between the two leaders and concentrate on their policies.

Trudeau and the more militant separatists may differ pragmatically on the usefulness of violence, on nationalism versus internationalism, but both Quebec and Canada are moving toward social radicalism. Lest one become confused by the confrontation politics, an historical perspective will remind us of the first objectives of the so-called "Quiet Revolution". There were differences over the base and space of operation, over strategy and tactics, but the objectives were socialism and radicalism. More than a decade ago Marcel Chaput, committed to the liberation of Quebec, concisely stated the differences and similarities between himself and Trudeau. "In the same way that *Cite Libre* wants the inward liberation of Quebec, Separatism (a word which I absolutely detest) wants outward liberation. Only the union of these two types can bring the real liberation of Quebec. ...*Cite Libre* and Separatism represent two complementary types of liberation necessarily linked to one another....Separatism is unacceptable if it doesn't lead to inward liberation. This isn't just a prophecy, either; it is the lucid acceptance of a necessary fact. The liberation of the French-Canadian nation demands a global solution...." 25)

In his drive for radical change, Trudeau has given priority to the democratic means of confrontation and has condemned violent change. The PQ victory indicates, according to him, that "democracy is in good health in Quebec, and that is good news."26) The merit of democracy may be that it permits radical change without radical violence. But what merit is there in democracy when it is used as a means of confrontation? What is the merit of a democracy if this political right can be exercised only at election time, every four or five years? What does it profit if Parliament is a means to transform parliamentary democracy? It is possible to use parliamentary democracy to destroy itself. (FFC, p.106) Canadians have never given their approval for such a democracy which is gradually replacing the traditional representative parliamentary democracy. Liberal democracy can be easily co-opted by those who do not wish or intend to work within the "spirit" of the system, or "play by the rules". People are beginning to realize that government by mandarins does not necessarily provide more freedom than government by mediocrities. (AP,p.24)

Even though Trudeau personally detested invoking the War Measures Act during the October Crisis, and set aside the constitutional liberties of innocent citizens, it provided him with extra-ordinary parliamentary powers, and with parliamentary approval at that. Only the NDP had the dogmatic determination to defend Parliament. Tommy C.Douglas, then NDP leader, said on CBC radio, October 16,1970: "But we are not going to defend democracy by having the government bypass Parliament and refuse to use the democratic means which it has at hand. If we want to demonstrate that democracy is more effective than violence, then, surely, we should be using the democratic procedure instead of that the government has taken under the sweeping War Measures Act." 27) Upon his retirement as Progressive Conservative leader, Robert Stanfield admitted that going along with the government's extreme measures rather than taking a firm stand in defence of parliamentary democracy was the greatest mistake in his political career. As Gellner foresaw, "if extraordinary powers can be assumed by government on as flimsy evidence of national danger as there was in October 1970, the same can happen again and again." And it happened again in October 1975 with the government's "emergency" wage and price controls, sanctioned this time not by the opposition parties, but by the Supreme Court on a technical question of federal-provincial powers. There is now a political and legal precedent to exercise extra-ordinary powers. What should be of concern to every citizen who appreciates freedom and liberal democracy, is that a federal Cabinet and a Supreme court of law decided, on the basis of flimsy evidence of an economic emergency, to override fundamental economic and political freedoms. Given the background of the individuals and the nature of the situation, continued confrontation and the politics of crisis can be expected between Ottawa and Quebec. As reported, the federal government has requested the reassignment of a military unit to Ottawa - not, in our opinion, for civil war, but to back up extra-parliamentary "emergency" powers. In a hysterical climate of crisis, in the urgency of "saving" Canada, Parliament and/or the Supreme Court may readily grant "emergency" powers to the Prime Minister. A country which continually experiences the politics of confrontation and a government which resorts to extra-parliamentary powers, will witness that the strength of its parliamentary democracy is rapidly eroded.

Ironically, the use of the War Measures Act reminds one of Trudeau's condemnation of the use of the 1949 Riot Act in Quebec. He wrote: "In law, the reading of this Act is an emergency measure, the purpose of which is to achieve the immediate dispersal of a rioting crowd... they arrested these people, who were in no way in a state of riot, without giving them the time or the opportunity to disperse; they also arrested other people who were not even assembled, but who were simply present in restaurants, in their homes, or on the sidewalks; and they had the nerve to leave the Act in effect for 53 hours! " (AS, p.331)

In retrospect, few Canadian intellectuals in Canada have contributed more to undermining respect for higher law and supreme authority than Trudeau. He has written that authority and freedom are not received from God and do not reside in laws of nature. He has rationalized revolt, boycotts, illegal strikes, student demonstrations; in short, mass civil disobedience. He has placed his conscience above the law. His reason is the highest authority. While he is not personally responsible for the actions of other individuals or groups, strikers, students, or self-styled anarchists, he can be held accountable for contributing to the spirit of lawlessness by undermining the foundations of traditional authority.

Trudeau has remained consistent to his secular theory on civil disobedience throughout the decades. Even as Prime Minister, he joined two colleagues to send a telegram in the Spring of 1975 to striking Asbestos workers, pledging "our solidarity with our Asbestos comrades." On the opening day of Parliament (October 12, 1976) he did not cross the picket lines of *The Canadian Press*, who were on strike. On the Day of Protest (October 14, 1976) the workers protested his controls program by practising his theory of civil disobedience. (AP. pp.34,36,82)   With Trudeau's concept of authority, which removed the moral foundations, it is not "surprising that we are reaping that harvest today in Quebec (and Canada) where every union leader, every leader of small groups says, 'Well, why should we respect established order?' "28) The eventual harvest is not more democracy, but extra-ordinary powers, not more freedom, but greater authoritarian control over society. The late political theorist Hanna Arendt wrote: "The defiance of established authority, religious and secular, social and political, as a world-phenomenon may well one day be accounted the outstanding event of the last decade."29)

Notes

1. Andre Laurendeau, **Witness for Quebec,** pp. 161,162.
2. Quoted in Marcel Chaput, **Why I am a Separatist,** p. 84.
3. Fernand Dumont, "The Systematic Study of the French-Canadian Total Society," in Marcel Rioux and Yves Martin, eds. **French-Canadian Society,** pp. 390-391.
4. In the words of Lenin, "The masses learn from practical life and not from books...." Stefan T. Possony, ed., **Lenin Reader,** p. 397. Mao had similar thoughts when he stated: "I advise those of you who have only book knowledge and as yet no contact with reality, and those who have little practical experience, to recognize their own shortcomings and become a bit more humble." Stuart R. Schram, The Political Thought of Mao Tse-tung, p. 118.
5. Joseph Schumpeter, **Capitalism, Socialism and Democracy,** pp. 153-154.
6. P.E. Trudeau, Politique fonctionnel, Cite Libre (June 1950), p. 21
7. Quoted in F. Scott and Michael Oliver, eds., **Quebec States her Case,** pp. 138-139.
8. Martin Sullivan, **Mandate '68,** p. 240.
9. Donald Peacock, **Journey to Power,** p. 210.
10. Peacock, **op. cit.,** pp. 367-377.

11. **Canadian News Facts,** 1968, Vol. 2, No. 14, p. 116.
12. Quoted in Sullivan, **op. cit.,**p. 317.
13. Possony, ed., **op. cit.,** p. 475.
14. **Ibid.,** p. 468.
15. **Ibid.,** pp. 430-431. Some "anarchists" got the message. Pierre Vallieres had taken over from Trudeau the editorship of **Cite Libre.** He was the FLQ's "apostle" of violence. After the 1970 October Crisis, Vallieres now confessed his dislike for violence and preference for democratic means to achieve a socialist Quebec. Like Trudeau, he is still committed to radical change in society.
16. John Gellner, **Bayonets in the Streets,** pp. 102, 125.
17. **The Telegraph Journal,** March 8, 1976, p. 1.
18. Quoted in **The Globe and Mail,** October 2, 1976, p. 1. In the well-received speech at the Liberal Policy Convention, March 23-26, 1977, Lemelin said that the Parti Quebecois is led "by a hard-core group of intellectuals bitten by the bug of such European ideological fantasies as self-determination, independence, Marxism, socialism..." Roger Lemelin "An Ill-fitting Imported Ideology Won't Suit Canada," **The Globe and Mail,**March 26, 1977, p. 10. However, "social radicalism" is also an imported ideology which is proving to be ill-suited for Canadian unity. As Lemelin said: "All those high risk transplants come to a high price... in the beautiful garden of the just society."
19. Lemelin wrote: "Why I Support Pierre Elliott Trudeau," in **Le Devoir and Quebec's L'Action,** March 26, 1968, and paid for an interview with Trudeau on Montreal TV. He reassured the Quebec bishops " he's okay. " Sullivan, **op. cit.,** p. 322. He even told Trudeau to use teeth whiting — not white whiskey — to win elections.
20. **The Toronto Star,** November 27, 1976, p. 1.
21. **Maclean's,** January 10, 1977, p. 10.
22. **Maclean's,** November 1, 1976, p. 14.
23. Quoted in **The Montreal Star,** November 20, 1976.
24. **Maclean's,** January 10, 1977, p. 4.
25. Chaput, **op. cit.,** p. 85. In the Foreword Chaput wrote: "Any of you who long for a real Canadian Constitution, you are a Separatist. The only difference between you and me is that you want Canada to be free in relation to England and the United States, and I want Quebec to be free in relation to Canada."p. iv. Like Levesque, Chaput detests the word Separatist, but his publisher, Jacques Hebert, insisted on a "cut up" maple leaf on the cover. He claims Canada never was a unity.
26. True, the PQ's majority, for example, has removed the need for the existence of and use of violence by the FLQ, which stated in its Manifesto: "The separatist political parties will never gain sufficient power to overcome the colonizers' political and economic hold." Frank Scott and Michael Oliver, eds., **op. cit.,** p. 86.
27. **Canadian News Facts,** 1970, Vol. 4, No. 9, p. 531.
28. **Maclean's,**October 20, 1975, p. 6.
29. Hanna Arendt, "Civil Disobedience," in **The Crisis of the Republic,** p. 69, New York: Harcourt, Brace Jovanovich, 1972.

"Above all, it is our determined wish to make government more accessible to people, to give our citizens a sense of full participation in the affairs of government...."
Trudeau, 1968

"But I still see the job as one in which no government can do anything that people can't be instructed or be educated to accept.... People want to be led...."
Trudeau, 1975

Chapter 3
Participatory Democracy

Parliamentary government has served Canada well for over one hundred years. In this representative form of democracy, Canadians participate through their constituency parties and their representatives in Parliament. Over the years, there have been minor changes in political traditions, rules and procedures of Parliament, but with the advent of Prime Minister Trudeau, there have been reforms which fundamentally transformed Parliament. Representative democracy has been pushed aside in favour of a radically different form of government called "participatory democracy". Trudeau's perception of leadership is integral to his conception of participatory democracy, both within the Liberal Party and for the country.

According to radical theorists, representative democracy through a parliament favoured special interest groups and prevented direct participation by the people. The critical theorists called for a "true" democracy, direct people's democracy, a participatory democracy in which the people would be able to take direct action in industrial, educational, and governmental decisions. The introduction of participatory democracy through Parliament means the inevitable end of Parliament as a liberal representative body and as a meaningful institution for decision-making.

Liberal Leadership

In the early fifties, Trudeau was a leading figure in a group of anti-nationalist, socialist intellectuals who published the *Cite Libre* magazine, dedicated to the overthrow of the Duplessis regime and the democratization of Quebec. Instead of joining the Liberal Party in this objective, Trudeau and others organized the Rassemblement, with the goal to build "a movement of education and democratic action." Trudeau sought to unite the opposition forces under the slogan: "Democracy first.... After that it will be up to the sovereign people to opt freely for the choices they prefer." (FFC,p.x) It is common for radical leaders around the world to use the slogan "democracy first", and only afterwards do the people discover what was really meant by the term "democracy". In Quebec, the union des forces democratiques under the leadership of Trudeau and the Rassemblement group, came to naught due to ideological quarreling and the success of the Quebec Liberal Party in the early sixties.

When the Liberals united all the opposition forces in 1960, the *Cite Libre* group "was notably absent." (AP, p.17) They were not about to sink their identity in the Liberal Party. After all, Trudeau's theme was not liberalism, but "democracy first". For him, the Liberal Party was a Party of private interest groups which did little to cultivate democracy in Quebec. (FFC, p.120) Consequently, he pledged to support the Parti Socialiste Democratique, the Quebec wing of the C.C.F. (AP, pp.11, 17) He formed a united front with the newly formed New Democratic Party (NDP) and promised to campaign for socialist candidates. In 1963, Trudeau campaigned for his friend, Charles Taylor, the NDP candidate in Mount Royal. In 1965, he ran against him as a Liberal. Trudeau never joined the NDP because "most of its Quebec followers were in fact exchanging socialism for nationalism" (FFC, p.xx) and the class struggle into a nationalist struggle of the French fact in Quebec. (FFC, pp.151-171)

The experiences from 1956 to 1965, according to Ramsay Cook, "probably taught Trudeau that founding a new party was far more difficult than assuming control of an old one."(AP, p.18) In *Social Purpose for Canada* (1961), Trudeau presented a "pragmatic approach to strategy" for socialists in Canada. He passionately argued for a more realistic strategy and variety of tactics by socialists and fewer doctrinaire positions on means. "My plea is merely for greater realism and greater flexibility in the socialist approach to problems of federalism." (FFC, p.125) The same appeal for realism was the main thrust of the 1964 "Canadian Manifesto" signed by Trudeau, among others. Trudeau's flexibility and sense of realism is demonstrated in his affiliation with the Liberal Party. It would be easier to seek the leadership in a party which was flexible in philosophy (liberal pragmatism) than in a new party which was doctrinaire about its socialism. He apparently decided on the strategy of working from within the Liberal Party.

There are commentators who interpret his membership in the Liberal Party to mean that Trudeau became a liberal. They confuse strategy with political philosophy. In 1965, the Liberal Party in Quebec subordinated its identity by taking in Pierre Trudeau, Jean Marchand and Gerard Pelletier. These men entered the Party on their terms. The Liberal Party desperately desired Marchand, but he insisted on including the other two and that Trudeau be secured a safe riding because many constituency ridings refused to accept Trudeau as their Liberal candidate. It is not surprising considering what he had said about the Liberals and the Party leadership shortly before he joined. In 1963 he still promised to campaign for the NDP and defeat "Pope Pearson" because Pearson had permitted American missiles in Canada. In addition, he was "concerned with the anti-democratic reflexes of the spineless Liberal herd" who followed Pearson "with the elegance of animals heading for the trough...."2) A decade later, professional Party Liberals were still frustrated with Trudeau. In the wake of the near defeat in the 1972 election, they went to see him in the winter of 1973. One of the participants told Trudeau: "You cannot be horse and jockey." A campaign chairman was required to be the jockey. Did they control him or he manipulate them? According to Christina Newman's account, "they learned his tricks and he learned theirs." One participant at the winter meeting remembers controlling his anger at Trudeau, saying to himself, "he's been our leader for five years and he still doesn't know what the party is all about."3)

Christina Newman wrote that, during the 1974 election, Trudeau finally joined the Party after six years as its leader. But as an expert politician, Trudeau needed no "politicizing". If he had become a liberal at heart, perhaps she should have written about the "liberalization" of Pierre. What really occurred during those six years was the radicalization of the Liberal Party. This is possible because, as Christina Newman added herself, "Canadian liberalism is an ideology as malleable as Silly Putty." A decade earlier, Trudeau stated it more precisely. "The political philosophy of the Liberal Party is simplicity itself. Say anything, think anything you like. But put us in power because we are best fitted to govern...What idiots they all are...."4) Trudeau was well qualified to govern, but he considered his 1968 leadership candidacy a "huge practical joke on the Liberal Party."5) As he hinted, if the press had really known him, the Liberal Party might not have taken him. But the Party and the press, with few exceptions, did not take Trudeau seriously at his word and in the context of his pre-Liberal days. The Liberal's choice in 1968 of Pierre Trudeau may be pragmatism at work, but Trudeau's choice of the Liberal Party in 1965 was pragmatic in strategy, not in philosophy. He has never publicly renounced his earlier commitment to "social radicalism". (AS, p.343)

Right from the start, Trudeau has sought to give the Liberal Party a turn to the Left. During the years in which Trudeau has been the leader, he has radicalized the Party, given it a new direction (by means of a new definition of "liberalism"), a new "dimension" and a different conception of democracy. The principles of the re-oriented Party and government are an "ongoing process", according to Trudeau, because the principles of liberalism must evolve in a changing world, advancing liberalism beyond itself. He told the 1970 Liberal Policy Convention: "No other form of change is worthy of men who have evolved, through liberal thought, to that level at which a growing proportion of mankind claims to function." (CC, p.87) It is his belief that the world's people are moving towards the Left. (AS, p.339) In 1968, when he sought the leadership, he did not give the Party's definition of liberalism, but his philosophy of liberation. "Liberation is the only philosophy for our time...because it is prepared to experiment and innovate and because it knows that the past is less important than the future."6) In 1970, he challenged the Party "to face its own ideal, to re-examine its own tenets and policies, and pronounce its views on the direction which it proposes this country should take."(CC, p.65) He pleaded for the tolerance of liberals, flattering them that they were so tolerant - tolerant of his ideas and policies. What about the life-long members and leaders who want the Party to remain true to its traditional, liberal principles? He told the delegates to the Policy Convention in 1970 that a "passive liberal reclining on the cushions of the liberal tradition is as worthless and ineffective as any spiritless conservative." (CC, p.87) Such liberals are left behind while others re-examine Party tenets and policies.

The Party was going to be more than a constituency Party, representative of Liberals. No longer was it to be a party like the other parties in which the constituency passes resolutions "intended either to bind or to guide their leaders and caucuses in the coming months." It must be a party "which reaches out to absorb the ideas and to reflect the aspirations of all Canadians...the widest possible participation by those interested in questions of public policy." The 1969 Harrison Hot Springs Liberal Policy Conference was not a conference limited to Liberal Party members, but a thinkers' conference of Canadians from many national associations. It was not so much a partisan as a people's conference. It appears that one objective was to turn the Liberal Party into a national people's party.7)

In their enthusiasm for the new politics of the new leader, many Liberals were excited about participating, passing resolutions which would be sent on as policy guidelines for the Prime Minister and his Cabinet. Liberal Party members continued to think of participatory democracy in their own terms of liberal representative democracy. Of course, in this sense Trudeau's participatory democracy was "not merely a misnomer, but a monstrous fraud."8) According to Stewart, "The Prime Minister does not believe in participatory democracy, but in leadership democracy, and among his confidants he makes no bones about it."9)   Unfortunately, Stewart misunderstands the principle and misplaces the emphasis. From a radical theoretical perspective, leadership democracy is a manifestation of participatory democracy. Lenin's participatory democracy was a new leadership democracy, better known as "democratic centralism". This radical idea of participatory democracy helps explain Trudeau's approach. Democracy is important, but leadership is all important. This is also Joseph Schumpeter's view of democracy in which the people do not primarily decide issues, but only elect representatives. He wanted to leave lots of room for the vital fact of leadership and believed that the electorate does not normally control its political leaders in any way except by refusing to re-elect them. The true function of the electorate's vote is the acceptance of leadership. Similarly, Trudeau believes that "If the people are not pleased with what I have done then they can vote me out in the next election." (FFC,p.xxvi)

Elsewhere Trudeau has written that liberal democracy "genuinely demonstrates its faith in man by letting itself be guided by the rule of fifty-one percent."(AP, p.88) But neither Trudeau nor his confidants have this liberal faith in the people. At the 1969 Liberal Policy Conference, Marc Lalonde, then the Prime Minister's principal secretary, speaking about the role of delegates in a democracy, said: "People in riding associations don't have the sophisticated knowledge required. They're uninformed...."10) Trudeau himself told the delegates: "A party's principal concern should not be how to settle a particular strike - let the Minister of Labour and the Cabinet worry about that. It should be to resolve the continuing crisis in industrial relations by working out a better system of reconciling the interests of labour, management and the public. The task is not only more difficult, it is much more important."11) But if the people do not even have the sophisticated knowledge to recommend a solution to a particular strike, how can Lalonde expect the people to have the philosophical knowledge "to resolve the continuing crisis in industrial relations"? Suppose 75% of the delegates wanted a certain wage and price policy which was contrary to the social philosophy of the Prime Minister? "If that happened, Lalonde said, it would indicate that the government had not done a good job of explaining its policies; the need was not to change them, but to improve communications."12) Trudeau recognized "that one person may be right and ninety-nine wrong." (AP,p.88) Apparently, he believed that he was right and that it was necessary to persuade the ninety-nine "lost" Liberals to change their point of view. Since 1969 he has tried tactfully to persuade the Liberal Party of his radical idea of economic democracy which he envisioned during and in the *Asbestos Strike.* (AS, p.339) In 1976 it was presented as the framework of the working paper, *The Way Ahead*.

Participatory democracy, as Trudeau has developed it, gives the people more opportunity to talk and less direct influence on policy. At the 1969 thinkers' conference, he compared the Liberal Party members to airplane pilots. "We are like the pilots of a supersonic airplane. By the time an airport comes into the pilot's field of vision, it is too late to begin the landing procedure. Such planes must be navigated by radar." (CC, p.72) The members of the Liberal Party do not make the decisions because the flight plan originates from the Prime Minister under the radar supervision of the Prime Minister's Office. The exclusive and powerful Priorities and Planning Committee decided on *The Government's Priorities* in the summer of 1975, which was then passed on to the full Cabinet, but not to all Liberal members of Parliament. It was leaked to *The Toronto Star* to coincide with the Liberal Policy Convention in November 1975, but the report was not even available, let alone discussed or debated. The philosophical framework and new direction for Liberal policy have been decided from above. Afterwards, Parliament and the people are consulted and encouraged to participate in discussion and dialogue to persuade the public of the need for implementation of specific policies. As one active Ontario Liberal wrote: the "Party has no influence on the parliamentary wing. In my opinion, democracy within the Party has increased in the last four years but the Party's influence upon the parliamentary wing (Cabinet and PMO) - the true centre of power - has decreased sharply." 13) That is precisely the outcome of participatory leadership democracy: democracy from below and leadership from above.

Trudeau does not mind policy conventions, but he strongly resists leadership conventions to review his Party and parliamentary leadership. At the 1969 Policy Convention, Trudeau told the delegates that it "would be misleading to consider the conference as a test of authority over the Party or as a contest for power within it." He held the power in it and sought to extend his philosophy over it. He has successfully survived a vote on a leadership convention on three occasions. Even after he had set aside civil liberties in October 1970, only 11% of the delegates to the Policy convention voted for a leadership convention, and only 9% in 1973 after the 1972 Liberal losses. Although there was considerable opposition to Trudeau's leadership in 1975, heavy pressure was put on the delegates to vote down a leadership review and only 19% voted for a review. Trudeau's decision to impose controls after Finance Minister John Turner's resignation, and before the Policy convention, was a shrewd political move. A Cabinet minister said: "I shudder to think what the leadership vote would have been without the controls policy." 14) In voting down a leadership review, the Liberal Party members have removed the only real opportunity of democratic control over the centralized leadership. If the Party had voted for a review in 1975, the fortunes of the Liberals might have been brighter in 1976.

After eight years as Prime Minister, Trudeau has failed to unify the nation - one of his highest priorities as PM. The victory of the Parti Quebecois and defeat of the Quebec Liberal government illustrated his inability to rally his own province behind his policies. Morale within the federal Liberal Party is almost as low as its standing in the polls. But Trudeau is ready to fight both for his position as leader and for his policies. In October 1976 he told the Ontario Liberal caucus policy conference: "We have to worry, as Liberals, about the future of the Liberal Party. I'm beseeching the caucus to go out and organize and organize and organize again.... We may be running out of time....We mustn't worry about being popular, but must worry about being right." However, Liberals begin to realize that Trudeau is neither right, nor popular. With his left-of-liberal leadership, some worry that they may be left without a liberal society and the traditional Liberal Party - which was largely the case in Quebec and the West at the end of 1976. Trudeau may not be a liberal jockey, but he could be a Trojan horse within the Liberal Party and a Liberal Parliament. A decade before he accepted the Liberal leadership, he wrote: "...a prime minister 'gives himself' to his country....But it does not necessarily follow that such a gift is always to the advantage of the recipients: there are some gifts one would do well not to accept, as the Trojans learned to their cost some years ago." (AP, p.64) If Trudeau successfully continues to re-orient and evolve the Liberal Party towards the left, the NDP may look like a reactionary party, but the traditional Liberal Party may end up on the "scrap-heap" of history.

Parliamentary Democracy

Not only did Trudeau guide the Liberal Party into a new direction, but he also placed high priority on reform of the parliamentary system. At first glance, some of the reforms appeared to be necessary improvements. However, the final results were not always favourable.

Immediately after assuming the Party leadership, Prime Minister Trudeau stated in an election pamphlet, "Above all, it is our determined wish to make government more accessible to people, to give our citizens a sense of full participation in the affairs of government, and full control over their representatives."15) In the first Throne Speech of September 12, 1968, Trudeau claimed that participatory democracy would permit "the people of Canada a continuing, informed, and more active participation in the activities of their government." The newly elected parliamentarians should have realized that a side effect would be a decrease in their representative role. Direct communication with the constituents, via newly created regional desks in the PM's office, was a practical proposal to control the behaviour of the politicians, and effectively reduced the role of MPs by simply by-passing these elected representatives of the people.

Participatory democracy was devised as a means to turn a representative liberal system into a direct "people's democracy." Walter Stewart wrote that Trudeau "doesn't understand what parliamentary democracy is all about." He added: "his inability to grasp the role of that institution threatens to destroy it."16) However, it is precisely because Trudeau understood the traditional parliamentary system so well that he sought to reform it. He realized that representative democracy was not in accord with his concept of "participatory democracy" and he must, therefore, transform Parliament. Unfortunately, some political scientists have not been able to place Trudeau's actions into the total picture of his philosophy and goals. Some perceive the transformation of parliamentary government as a change to a presidential system. Denis Smith, formerly of Trent University, maintains the Canadian Prime Minister, in fact, has become as powerful as an American President. 17) They have empirically researched a shift in power from Parliament to the Cabinet and the Prime Minister. This trend could become the new norm for the structure of government in Canada. Smith's analogy is false, because the PM is far more powerful than any American president, particularly during the years of an absolute parliamentary majority. Even though President Kennedy waged a guerrilla war abroad and President Johnson faced a civil war situation at home, neither President would have dared to set aside civil liberties of the peaceful and more violent protestors. Soon after the War Measures Act was imposed by Trudeau, a U.S. Defence Department official told Walter Stewart: "You guys sure know how to keep the punks in line; we'd never dare try that. " 18) In neither theory nor practice did Trudeau act like an American President.

The degradation of Parliament rested on an historical misconception among political scientists of the classical parliamentary model in which the House of Commons was supposedly more powerful than the Cabinet and Prime Minister. But the latter constituted the executive power within the overall legislative authority of Parliament. In Representative Government (1860), the liberal John Stuart Mill delegated the preparation of legislation to the selected few (e.g.PM and Cabinet) reserving for the rest of the people's representatives, in particular the loyal opposition, the responsibility to watch and control Cabinet government. Parliament was a "congress of opinions", the politicians representing the public's opinion. A liberal Parliament was a government by public opinion, through representatives, and based on the respect for the opinions of the ordinary citizens.

However, for Trudeau, the "only constant factor to be found in my thinking over the years has been opposition to accepted opinions." He considered the "tyranny of public opinion" one of the worst offenders. "For public opinion seeks to impose its domination over everything. Its aim is to reduce all action, all thought, and all feeling to a common denominator." (FFC, pp. xix, xxi) Trudeau did not really believe in a liberal democracy, in which ordinary citizens through their MPs lead the nation. He acted more like an extra-parliamentary figure who considered himself under no obligation to respect the wishes of the people, or their elected officials.

Why, then become involved in the politics of such an obsolete parliamentary body? Is it true that he "ain't gonna need this House no longer"? 19) No, he needed to provide legitimacy for his radical programs, and if he could manage it, he was going to serve longer than any previous PM. That was why he gave such priority to changing the rules of Parliament. Through Parliament he could change society as he had so clearly stated. "The control period will...give us the necessary time to reform our economic institutions, our attitudes and public policies.... A call for an immediate start on a national reassessment of our values, our economic institutions... to adapt our attitudes and habits to the facts of life."20) He planned to bring about changes "in discussion with Parliament and the people...."

In order to understand the direction of Trudeau's thought and action more fully, it is helpful to note Lenin's important distinction between "historically obsolete" and "politically obsolete". In reply to the question: Should we participate in bourgeois parliaments? Lenin said: "Parliamentarism has become 'historically obsolete' That is true as regards propaganda. But everyone knows that this is still a long way from overcoming it practically...Parliamentarism is 'historically obsolete' from the standpoint of world history...Is parliamentarism 'politically obsolete'? That is quite another matter. It has been proved that participation in a bourgeois-democratic parliament even a few weeks...actually helps it to prove to the backward masses why such parliaments deserve to be dispersed; it helps their successful dispersal, and helps bourgeois parliamentarism to become 'politically obsolete'''.21) Likewise, Trudeau believed that it was practical and pragmatic to prove to the Canadian people that Parliament must either perform or perish; to perform it must transform. In a House of Commons debate (July 24,1969) he said: ''It will adapt or it will perish...at this time in history legislative institutions which fail to reform themselves do so at peril of their own destruction.'' It is interesting to note that he constantly drew attention to the ''new realities'' and that we must be in tune with the march of history. He simply stated that ''at this time in history'' institutions, attitudes and values must change without ever proving that we do live in a new economic era and that history is moving in only one direction. That narrow view of history helps explain why he has great difficulty empathizing with the desire for separatism in Quebec.

There is an important difference between reforming the rules of debate and transforming the institution, the parliamentary system. Genuine reforms, such as regular annual sessions, streamlining the schedule of weekly sessions, and committee assignments, can readily be agreed upon. However, some of the proposed reforms went to the heart of the liberal parliamentary body, in particular the proposals to change the Question Period and the timetable to debate legislation. Trudeau apparently considered these ancient parliamentary safeguards as historically obsolete, in need of reform, in order to make Parliament relevant and able to meet the needs of a new industrial society. ''We no longer live in a static world: we must go forward with the caravan of humanity or perish in the desert of time past.'' (AS, p.345)

Any reform which curtails or reduces the Question Period fundamentally alters liberal parliamentary government. Unrehearsed questioning of ministers, freely on any day, is an essential safeguard to maintain democratic control over the Cabinet and government bureaucracies. ''For decades, Question Period has been a time of salutary terror for governments, even those with huge majorities.'' 22) The new rules of rotation of ministerial attendance, and written questions in advance, to be answered much later, have ''largely defused'' the Question Period. 23)

Unlimited debate has been an essential principle in liberal parliamentary democracy. Trudeau sought to change all that by introducing the rule that, if the parties could not agree on limiting debate, the government's House leader would determine the timetable. The opposition parties felt so strongly on this principle, that they were willing to swallow the other reforms in order to stand firm on this point. When the House passed the less objectionable rule reforms, the Prime Minister gleefully stated that the limited debate proposal had been purposefully made objectionable as a ploy to achieve the other reforms. " We pulled the ground out from under them, and Parliament has a completely new set of rules...done by unanimous agreement." 24) However, the same objectionable proposal was back the following summer, in a more subtle form, but with fundamentally the same purpose, namely, that the government determines the timetable. In short, debates would be limited as a matter of principle. However, one of the great safeguards of freedom and democracy, according to the liberal J.S. Mill, is the right of MPs to talk and talk, and talk a government out of action: unlimited debate. But Trudeau became frustrated by a filibuster, because he believed in unlimited government action.

During the heated summer debate of 1969, Trudeau gave the opposition members a piece of his mind. "I think we should encourage members of the opposition to leave. Everytime they do, the I.Q. of this House rises considerably. The opposition seems to think it has nothing else to do but talk. That is all they have to do. They do not have to govern, they have only to talk. The best place in which to talk, if they want a forum, is, of course Parliament. When they get home, when they get out of Parliament, when they are fifty yards from Parliament Hill, they are no longer Honourable Members. They are just nobodies."25) At the November 1969 Liberal Convention he called Parliament a "Coney Island shooting gallery". In 1963 Trudeau had called Liberal members idiots. In power as PM, he criticized opposition members for what Marx called "parliamentary idiotism". Before his rise to power, Trudeau wrote: "I choke with indignation at the humiliations inflicted on that opposition. The point is that in a parliamentary democracy the opposition is the last and most important bulwark against arbitrary tyranny; through it the people reserve the right to criticize from moment to moment the way they are governed - through it they nip legislative and adminstrative abuses in the bud." (AP, p. 79) What happened to his view of the lofty role of the opposition and, through it, the power of the people? He even sharply reduced the ability of the opposition to use the parliamentary principle of calling for a vote of confidence "from moment to moment." Part of the reform package was a limitation on the freedom of the opposition parties to call for a vote of confidence at any time.

At least one person, Lenin, has shown the way out of the dilemma. "The way out of parliamentarism is to be found, of course, not in the abolition of the representative institutions and the elective principle, but in the conversion of the representative institutions from mere 'talking shops' into working bodies." 26) Trudeau was not pleased with the long "holidays" of the MPs and the higher salary increases. He was determined to transform Parliament into an efficient working body. If he was to bring about "the new society we need to create", much legislation would be required. Parliamentary committees were given more work, but not more power. The power he kept for himself.

Trudeau's proposals sought to transform Parliament from a free institution of unlimited debate into a more efficient body. In the 1974 Throne Spreech he still pleaded for "more rational use of our time" and recommended that time for discussion be further reduced when Parliament dealt with "purely technical questions." But, as he well knew, there are no purely technical questions. The more technical questions of parliamentary rules and procedures are the most significant political questions, as the complex debate over the rules changes revealed. In the United Nations, for instance, there is potentially more political controversy and need for debate over technical questions of procedure than of policy. The procedural questions about how to amend the BNA Act outweigh the potential content of a new Canadian constitution. The Supreme Soviet of the USSR is the most efficient, but least liberal of parliamentary bodies. A liberal parliamentary body has always been a talking body, a debating society, where scoring "debating points" is at the heart of Parliamentary government. And as Harold Laski, the British intellectual labour leader and one of Trudeau's former teachers, has said: " The alternative to the 'talking shop' is the concentration camp. "27) The Liberal House Leader, Mitchell Sharp, arguing as a Liberal, said that the "opposition should not be able to bring the government to its knees by talking, but only by voting. "28) Columnist Walter Stewart suspected that by more rational use of time, the Prime Minister had in mind "not making the House of Commons work better for everybody, but making the opposition shut up." 29) Conservative members of the rules committee began to catch on. Conservative MP James McGrath said: "Every time the rules are changed, we get screwed. " 30)

A rational, liberal use of parliamentary time would be a far greater safeguard of freedom and democracy than the Prime Minister's rationale for "efficiency". In particular after the 1974 election, legitimacy, not efficiency, was the primary responsibility of modern democratic government. The fundamental question was not whether the Canadian people would obey the PM and his government, but whether or not he had the constitutional authority to embark on a radical transformation of Canadian society and structure of government without explicitly describing the type of society he hoped to create before election time. Trudeau had not abolished Parliament, but he had abdicated the spirit of liberal parliament-arism.

His estrangement from the liberal tradition was also manifested by his public disrespect. Should one be more shocked by phrases like: " that was your God-damned question"; "Why don't you shut up?"; "eat shit"; "fuddle duddle" and special status for Quebec as "une connerie" or by statements which illustrate his contempt for the people's representatives in Parliament, such as: "idiots"; "stupid filibuster"; "nobodies"? From a traditional perspective, the Prime Minister's obscene remarks reflect, according to Walter Stewart, "the careless contempt shown by the Prime Minister for the institution of Parliament, its traditions and rules." 31)

The new morality of "the new society" was manifested in Trudeau's attitude toward and treatment of scandals in his Cabinet. In the advanced stage of democracy, opposition parties should not spend their time dragging up scandals. "I don't think that at this sophisticated stage in our democracy people conceive of the opposition as merely a tool with which to find scandals in the ranks of the government or to level criticism or jibes at specific actions." 32) Such actions were inefficient because they hindered the process of passing legislation for the "new society".

In March 1975, two of the Cabinet Ministers were alleged to be guilty of parliamentary impropriety, interference with the judicial process. Public Works Minister C.M.Drury had the traditional sense of parliamentary integrity to resign. However, the Prime Minister refused to accept the resignation, to the great consternation of the opposition leaders. "Out of sheer disgust," said the parliamentarian Stanley Knowles, "I move that this House do now adjourn." Mr.Ed

Broadbent, Leader of the NDP, stated that Trudeau's stand was a "contempt of Parliament and contempt of law which effects all Canadians. We are not going to let a renegade government abuse that principle. " 33) *The Montreal Star's* editorial stated in the same issue that Trudeau "displayed contempt for Parliament and abandoned the elementary standards of government decency." On the CBC's "As It Happens" (March 15, 1976) program, Broadbent referred to the lack of respect for the rule of law which the PM had in the parliamentary tradition. Trudeau did not stand within the basic decency of liberal parliamentary standards. His philosophy of "liberation" had the basic tenet that the past is of minor importance. From this perspective, one can understand, even while disagreeing, why the Prime Minister so freely ignored parliamentary traditions and ethical standards.

Canada must move with "the caravan of humanity." Therefore, new rules and roles for Parliament were necessary for it to be politically relevant in "the new society" as Trudeau heralded in the new scientific industrial era of world history. Each and every proposal for parliamentary reform must be carefully evaluated in the light of different conceptions of Parliament: the liberal democratic versus the democratic socialist version. If not, the politicians will reform their legislative institution at the peril of their own obsolescence. In 1965 Trudeau stated that he did "not accord an absolute and eternal value to the political structures or the constitutional forms of states." (FFC, p.53) Walter Stewart summed up Trudeau's manipulations of Parliament well. "What is distressing in all the changes that have been made in Parliament during Trudeau's reign is that, instead of streamlining and strengthening the institution, they have curbed and weakened it... the Prime Minister has run it into a wall."34) The House of Commons lost its central place as the arena where new legislation is introduced. That now occurs in committee. There was little aura of excitement, there was little media interest and many MPs were bored by the mechanical passing of legislation. The powerlessness of committees is made abundantly clear by the Public Accounts Committee's inability to find out the truth about the agent fees in the sale of atomic reactors. The foreign policy debate (1968-69) is an example of how little influence the parliamentary wing had on the actual decision-making. It is an illustration of participatory democracy under Trudeau: consultation and reports, but no direct participation at the policy level. More details are presented in a following chapter.

When asked in April 1969 if he was satisfied with the political re-direction in Canada, Trudeau replied: "...I know the rudder is beginning to press against the waves and I know the ship is beginning to straighten her course. Perhaps the observer on the deck smoking his pipe sees the horizon much as it was and doesn't realize it, but perhaps he will find himself disembarking at a different island than the one he thought he was sailing for."35) Apparently Canadians are not aware of where the ship of state is heading. However, over a decade ago, he deplored the lack of a clearly defined direction by those in leadership positions. In a manifesto, which Trudeau signed in 1964, it was written: "Public figures, federal and provincial, do not provide the people with a clear idea of the direction in which they want the country to go." 36)

Decision-making has rapidly been shifted away from the people and their representatives in Parliament to the Prime Minister's Office. There may not be a Canadian or American way of decision-making, but there is a democratic and undemocratic way of decision-making. There is considerable difference between scientific planning by mandarins for freedom of the people and the people, via their representatives, planning their own freedom, making their own decisions. If the experience of the White House Staff under Kennedy, Johnson or Nixon is any guide, everybody believes in democracy until he gets to the top. By that time, democratic procedures are overshadowed by the desire to get things accomplished.

At one time Trudeau accused Quebec politicians of "outward acceptance of the parliamentary game, but without any inward allegiance to its underlying moral principles." (FFC, p.106) By providing Parliament with a completely new set of rules, Trudeau pulled the ground from under the loyal opposition.

Leadership Democracy

In the preceeding discussion on participatory democracy it has been shown that the people may participate, but have no decision-making power. Their role consists of discussions within a given framework, usually after basic policy has already been adopted. Trudeau's concept of "democracy" appears to be similar to that of Schumpeter; a vote means acceptance of leadership. The electorate votes in its leader(s), but has no right to seek control over their decision-making until the next election when it can vote in new leaders if not satisfied. Participatory democracy under Trudeau involved the concept of "leadership democracy".

There is little in Trudeau's academic and political background to indicate that he has any genuine appreciation of representative democracy, especially a traditional liberal conception of leadership. A liberal leader has, in principle, respect for the ordinary citizen, the rationality of the electorate and its representatives. Trudeau, on the other hand, referred to the people as "the horde" and the liberal people as a "liberal herd", as "animals heading for the trough". He referred to Liberal politicians as "idiots" and MPs as "nobodies". Opposition members had low I.Q.s and Liberal back-benchers are "trained donkeys". He rode roughshod over the vital traditions of parliamentary democracy. Public opinion becomes "tyranny". The Prime Minister spoke as if the people were demanding reform of Parliament, but that was not accurate. As Trudeau already stated in the 1968 Throne Speech, it is the view of the government, in other words, his view, " that Canadians feel that Parliament is too far removed from the people it serves....In order that parliamentary institutions may retain the confidence of the people... it is essential that provisions be made for legislative machinery that can act speedily on ...the growing parliamentary program of the future." By rapidly transforming the cherished institutions and traditions of Canadians, a crisis of confidence was inevitably created.

In an interview with Peter Newman, Trudeau said that the "role of a leader in a democratic society is to show the way to the people, but not to be out of touch with them, not to have theoretical ideas which the people are not able to accept at this particular time." 37) The notion that people want to be led is not a liberal concept in harmony with representative democracy. It is the tactical answer to the question: " Just how much reform can the majority of the people be brought to desire at the present time? " (FFC, p.127) Trudeau was highly conscious of being just "ahead" of the people - just to the left - not too far, and at that point lead them to accept his priorities and policies. It was from the above perspective that Trudeau's government developed policies. In the words of Prime Minister Trudeau, his government chose: "the areas where it wants to intervene and exercise its powers in an authoritarian way. That's a liberal approach, it's less authoritarian, I suppose, than a socialist approach, which theoretically at least, thinks that the state can decide better than the people." 38)

An examination of the actual decision-making process showed that the Prime Minister doggedly followed his own priorities and goals, and that his role in relation to the people was to explain and educate. He wanted to lead the people, but not push forward, a crucial distinction, theoretical concepts which the people are not capable of accepting. Trudeau placed great emphasis on a leader educating the people, making them believe that they want what he has in mind for them. This is not liberal representative democracy, but "leadership democracy". Throughout his years as Prime Minister, he has consistently been able to pursue his own goals in the areas of political and economic policy. Numerous examples come to mind, but perhaps the most detailed one is the foreign policy study by Thordarson. Would Trudeau not have to agree with his own words that "it is intolerable that one man should claim to know better than the majority what kind of social and political order is good for them." (AP,p.40)

Given the wide margin in favour of the image of Trudeau in the 1974 polls, especially in comparison with Robert Stanfield, leadership became the campaign issue, and not inflation where the Prime Minister had not yet provided decisive leadership. This approach was compatible with Trudeau's conception of democracy where leadership is the key element upon which the people vote. But, as the NDP leader, David Lewis, warned during the campaign: " Political leadership isn't a matter of a person. Political leadership is a matter of policy, of program, of philosophy, of attitude, of sensitivity. " 39) There was a concerted effort against the NDP and they lost many seats. 40)

In Trudeau's participatory leadership democracy, elections carry great significance. Has he responsibly presented the issues in order that the electorate be able to make an educated decision? In the 1974 campaign the people were persuaded to believe that Trudeau was not for wage and price controls. "Wage and price controls is not the answer," Trudeau told a Winnipeg audience (June 14, 1974). A speech was prepared for Ontario Liberal candidates which reiterated: "Wage and price controls aren't new.... Wage and price controls do not work." 41)   The Prime Minister successfully manipulated public opinion to vote for the Liberals (thus against wage and price controls). The election results were barely settled before he reactivated his pre-election contingency plans for wage and price controls. One is reminded of another sentence in the 1964 manifesto which Trudeau also signed which stated: "...the voters can never be sure of the relationship between what is said today and done tomorrow." 42) In short, the government did something which it had led the people to believe it would not do.

In the face of such a reversal of position, the only way he could impose his will was to exercise the politics of crisis by invoking "emergency" legislation in the name of "good government." However "good" the legislation may have been, it was a solution against which the Liberals had campaigned. Therefore, one could question the legitimacy of the government in a liberal democratic sense, a government which had spent millions to persuade the public that this was not the solution which they planned to use. It is one thing to spend private funds to campaign against controls, but quite another thing to consider it "perfectly defensible" to use more than a million dollars of taxpayers' money to advertise the imposition of legislation which Trudeau had criticized as unworkable during the election. The opposition parties in Parliament voted against the controls program. A Supreme Court may rule favourably on the technical legality, but does not judge the electoral morality of the legislation.

Aside from the question of legality, Canadians were concerned about the government's deception of the people and the consequent destruction of the democratic electoral process. Part of Prime Minister Trudeau's low standing in the polls of late 1976 arose out of the public's awareness that they had been manipulated. In a 1942 by-election, the politically active and youthful Trudeau campaigned against the immorality and the injustice of the federal government which had imposed conscription after promising not to do so. "So the Government has resorted to ruses such as the plebiscite and elevation of the General, a pro-conscription candidate to the Cabinet. This is all sickeningly dishonest...." 43) During the 1968 election Trudeau was heckled by some NDP supporters in Vancouver. He turned on the Tommy Douglas supporters and said: " You cannot tell lies to the people. They will not believe you. People are more sophisticated now. That is the thing we are discovering in this election - that the people do not want to be conned by any party. " 44) It appeared that there are still some who can deceive an electorate and get away with it, at least once.

The experience revealed more about the leader than the sophistication of the electorate. He may have resorted to ruses such as the elevation of restless backbenchers to the Cabinet, but one wonders how much he really cared for elections, how much he was theoretically and practically committed to a liberal democratic system of representative government. He did not hesitate to postpone two by-elections in 1975, preventing two ridings from being represented in Parliament for almost an entire year. Trudeau once strongly denounced similar actions. "When a prime minister refuses for four months to receive the delegates of twenty-one thousand university students who politely seek an interview, he is a bad servant and ought to be fired." (AP, p.65) St.John's West had gone unrepresented in Parliament for thirteen months and ten days - the longest period ever in Canadian history. At the time of the 1976 Christmas recess, six vacancies existed in the House. After recess, Health Minister Marc Lalonde told reporters that "it would not be responsible to hold them (by-elections) right away."

The Prime Minister provided leadership. In his words, "I know the ship is beginning to straighten her course." The problem lay in the fact that the leadership had hardly been democratic in the liberal parliamentary tradition. On the basis of his knowledge and close observation in Ottawa, Stewart wrote: "To all intents and purposes, Canada is no longer run by Parliament, or the cabinet, or even the party in power; it is run by the Prime Minister and his own personal power bloc."45)

The "Supergroup" surrounding the Prime Minister became the new elite. This unelected group of specialists advised the Prime Minister. Their close proximity to Trudeau lay not only in personal loyalty to the man, but also in their shared trust in science and technology to solve problems. One could say it was goverment with the advice and consent of the new scientific priesthood. This group had the primary input into the area of planning and priorities - the area which Trudeau had given top priority. Speaking to political science students at Carleton University, Jim Davey, the PM's programme secretary, explained in great detail how government really worked. Afterwards a graduate student asked the question: " I've heard you describing how our country is run for an hour and forty minutes and there are two words I have yet to hear you utter - Parliament and Cabinet. What happened to them?" 46)

The troublesome aspect of his leadership is that Trudeau presents one of his philosophic assumptions as fact, namely, that given the complexity and uncertainty in society, people cannot plan for themselves. Consequently, government must increasingly plan for them; euphemistically called planning for freedom. In addition, the planning should be done by a scientific, technical elite, who have the technical expertise, but limited know-how of the politics of planning. In relation to representative democracy, this planning group was beyond the reach of Parliament, and was responsible only to the PM. Under Trudeau, the MP's had less access to the Cabinet and absolutely none to the "supergroup" in planning and priorities. The Prime Minister has spoken eloquently on his strong commitment to counterweights. "I believe in the theory of counterweights. At every moment in time, I think each conscious servant of the public good must ask himself: in what direction should I be weighing in at this time?" Where was the counterweight to the unelected "supergroup" which operated largely in secret? Why not let Parliament have the role of planning, with input from the experts, in order that the people will be represented in this most crucial of areas in government?

Although the Prime Minister mentioned in a CTV interview (December 27, 1975) that there was no masterplan in his mind or in any group in the PM's Office, there had been a secret task force under the chairmanship of Michael Pitfield which had been planning the post-control policy for a new industrial society. The absolute secrecy at the top caused resentment among Liberal MPs and Cabinet ministers. There was no public, not even parliamentary input into this vital planning of the government's priorities, principles and strategies. What happened to representative democracy or even "participatory democracy"? As Herb Gray (Liberal-Windsor West) elaborated: "The secret task force does not provide in any way for the involvement in its work of the elected representatives of the Canadian people: it does not provide in any way for the involvement in its work of Parliament." 47) The 1964 manifesto also has some relevant passages on full information for the people. "Democratic progress requires the ready availability of true and complete information. In this way people can objectively evaluate their Government's policies. To act otherwise is to give way to despotic secrecy." 48) Mr. Gray, a former Minister of Consumer and Corporate Affairs, proposed to let the Canadian people in on "these big plans for their future" by setting up a special Parliamentary Committee on National Goals.

There was some similarity between the secrecy in Ottawa and that in the former Nixon White House. A top Canadian official told

Walter Stewart secretly that we now have a system where a non-elected Supergroup makes all the decisions. " What if we get, God save us, a Canadian Nixon? " 49) Michael J. Webb, Vice President of the Alberta Liberal Party, was reading Dan Rather's account of The Palace Guard and concluded, "This is happening here." He sent a copy to other Party leaders. 50) Several of Kennedy's and Johnson's trusted aides, such as Richard Goodwin and Joseph Califano had rejected as undemocratic the idea of a super White House staff, calling for its abolition. However, no such confessions have been forthcoming from the Canadian "supergroup" except from senior civil servants who were broken-hearted that their experienced, expert advice has been largely ignored. This is soul-destroying not only for the bureaucrats, but also for orderly democratic government.

The Prime Minister practiced leadership democracy on the principles of democratic centralism. He believed in consultation of the people, but decisions were presented from above. He listened to the pulse of the people, but planned policy from the top and then educated the people to accept it. In his 1976 Throne Speech Trudeau said: "Consultation ... means that the Goverment will place before interested Canadians its assessment of the major problems ... and its definition of the available options." In addition, he will pull all the stops in a move to educate the people to accept his policies and leadership. "But I still see the job as one in which no government can do anything that people can't be led to accept, can't be instructed or be educated to accept....I think the role of a leader in a democratic society is to show the way to the people....People want to be led....They have to be convinced that you are...consistently right. A great part of my job is getting people to accept that the goals as you see them are right." 51)   Between now and the next election, Canadians are going to be "led - instructed - educated - shown the way" and, possibly, "convinced".

As Stewart interpreted it: "Trudeau is the government; he is no longer the head of an administration, but its head, body and soul." 52) He became the total leader. Besides transforming Parliament into an extra-parliamentary body, he bypassed the regular party and bureaucratic channels and built his own party bureaucracy where all power was centralized. As Peter Cadeau, former director of Mitchell Sharp's Eglinton riding, wrote at the opening day of the 1975 Policy Convention, the Party "has become the obedient instrument for mandarin conceptions and advisory manipulations." Under Trudeau the Party became "more elitist than elective." 53) It was revealing that the theme of the 1975 Liberal Policy Convention was expressed in the first person: "The Canada that I want to build."

Media and academic men like John Harborn and Charles Taylor have mistakenly described Trudeau as the New Young Leader, symbolizing the liberal "consensus" image of politics.   But by academic training and political apprenticeship, Trudeau disciplined himself to be the young New Leader, the practitioner of the "politics of polarization and confrontation" in order to restructure radically the economy and society; as he has now set out to do. 54)

The traditional representative parliamentary system in Canada has been gradually reformed under the guise of efficiency and the slogan of participatory democracy. As Prime Minister, Trudeau shifted the spotlight of prestige and the power from the House of Commons to his office and committees. Both in the Liberal Party and in the nation, participatory democracy allowed much talk and discussion, but strictly confined within a given framework and without decision-making power. The resulting disillusionment has been particularly evident within the Liberal Party, but can be seen throughout the country.

Notes

1. Much of the background information comes from the introductions by Cook and Saywell. Quoted by Ramsay Cook, "The Coming of the Quiet Revolution," in **Approaches to Politics**, p. 15. and in John T. Saywell's Introduction to **Federalism and the French Canadians**, p. x.
2. Quoted by Douglas Stuebing, John Marshall and Gary Oakes, **Trudeau: A Man for Tomorrow**, p. 37.
3. Christina Newman, "Politicizing Pierre," **Maclean's**, October, 1974, pp. 36-42.

4. Quoted by Stuebing, Marshall and Oakes, **op. cit.**, p. 37.
5. Quoted in D. Peacock, **Journey to Power: The Story of a Canadian Election,** p. 227.
6. **Ibid** p. 293.
7. Thomas A. Hockin "Pierre Trudeau on the Prime Minister's Relations with Policy-Making Institutions and with His Party," in Thomas A. Hockin ed. Apex of Power: **The Prime Minister and Political Leadership in Canada,** pp. 146-149.
8. Walter Stewart, **Shrug: Trudeau in Power,** p. 88.
9. **Ibid.,** p. 103.
10. Quoted by Stewart, **op. cit.,** p. 92.
11. P.E. Trudeau, **Conversations with Canadians,** p. 72.
12. Quoted by Stewart, **op. cit.,** p. 93.
13. Quoted by Stephen Clarkson, "Pierre Trudeau and the Liberal Party," in Howard R. Penniman ed., **Canada at the Polls: The General Election of 1974,** p. 75.
14. Quoted in **Time,** November 24, 1975, p. 8.
15. Quoted in Stewart, **op. cit.,** p. 88. Italics removed.
16. **Ibid.,** pp. 146-148.
17. See "President and Parliament: The Transformation of Parliamentary Government in Canada," in Thomas A. Hockin ed., **op. cit.,**p. 308-325. In the same study, Joseph Wearing takes issue with Smith's misconception and writes: "A whole new perspective is provided if attention is focused on the Prime Minister's relationship to his Cabinet and through them to his party. In Canada, the office begins to look quite unpresidential — at least when the system is working well." **Ibid.,** p. 332. However, from the perspective of participatory leadership democracy, the office of the Prime Minister looks quite unparliamentary.
18. Stewart, **op. cit.,** p. 189.
19. **Ibid.,** p. 145.
20. Speech to Canadian Clubs of Ottawa, January 19, 1976.
21. Stefan T. Possony, ed., **Lenin Reader,** pp. 424-425, 428.
22. Stewart, **op. cit.,** p. 150.
23. **Ibid.,** p. 150.
24. **Ibid.,** p. 152.
25. House of Commons Debate, July 25, 1969, p. 11571.
26. Possony, ed., **op. cit.,** p. 196.
27. Quoted by John Diefenbaker, **Those Things We Treasure,** p. 7.
28. Quoted in **Maclean's,** July 12, 1976, p. 23.
29. **Maclean's,** January 1975, p. 6.
30. Quoted in **Maclean's,** July 12, 1976, p. 23.
31. Stewart, **op. cit.,** p. 148.
32. P.E. Trudeau, **Conversation with Canadians,** p. 73.
33. Quoted in **The Montreal Star,** March 13, 1976, p. 2.
34. Stewart, **op. cit.,** p. 159.
35. **The Best of Trudeau,** p. 36.
36. "An Appeal for Realism in Politics," **The Canadian Forum,** Vol. XLIV,

No. 520, p. 31.

37. **Maclean's,** October 20, 1975, p. 8.
38. **Ibid.**
39. **The Toronto Globe and Mail,** May 27, 1974.
40. In 1974 the Prime Minister personally started his national campaign in the riding of David Lewis, and ended up by defeating not only Lewis, but decimated the NDP by half. On election night, in the midst of personal defeat, David Lewis warned: "I hope for the sake of Canada that Trudeau will not return to the kind of attitude he had last time he had a majority government."
41. Quoted by Stephen Clarkson, "Pierre Trudeau and the Liberal Party — The Jockey and the Horse," in **Canada at the Polls.** H.R. Penniman, ed. pp. 82,87.
42. "An Appeal for Realism in Politics," p. 31.
43. Quoted in Stuebing, **op. cit.,** p. 17.
44. Quoted in Peacock, **op. cit.,** p. 357.
45. Stewart, **op. cit.,** p. 175.
46. **Ibid.,** p. 174.
47. **The Financial Post,** April 10, 1976, p. 7.
48. **An Appeal for Realism in Politics,"** p. 32.
49. Stewart, **op. cit.,** p. 189.
50. **Maclean's,** February 23, 1976, p. 56.
51. **Maclean's,** October 20, 1975, p. 8.
52. Stewart, **op. cit.,** p. 5.
53. **The Toronto Star,** November 7, 1975, p. B4.
54. See Charles Taylor, **The Pattern of Politics,** pp. 2-4.

"Federalism must be welcomed as a valuable tool ... from which the seed of radicalism can slowly spread."
Trudeau, 1961

"I am not in a frantic hurry to change the constitution simply because I am in a frantic hurry to change reality."
Trudeau, 1965

"The [erroneous] ... liberal idea of property helped to emancipate the bourgeousie but is now hampering the march towards economic democracy."
Trudeau, 1961

Chapter IV
Federalism, Constitution, and Human Rights

The years ahead will be a time of crucial political priorities and decision-making. Prime Minister Trudeau has renewed his challenge on bringing the Constitution to Canada. It is anticipated that he will seek to entrench his views on federalism, economic democracy and human rights in the revised Constitution. Given his almost total consistency over three decades, a review of his earlier writings will clarify recent and forthcoming actions of the Prime Minister.

Radicalism Through Federalism

Some have written that Trudeau's dogmatic commitment to federalism has proven to be a disastrous failure. However, such writers have overlooked one crucial fact: for Trudeau, federalism was only viewed as a means to achieve radical changes in society.

Trudeau has not been an uncritical defender of cooperative federalism. In his 1961 essay, "The Practice and Theory of Federalism," he did not so much make a case for federalism, but a case for radicalism through federalism. As a "democratic socialist", Trudeau was teaching social democrats of the NDP type to be pragmatic in their strategy and tactics for introducing socialism in Canada. The essay was an effort in "socialist education" first published in *Social Purposes for Canada* . As the editor, Michael Oliver, pointed out, the publication "coincides with the founding of a new political party which will inherit the traditions of the CCF. But it would be incorrect to assume that there is a direct connection between the New Party and the book." 1)

As a matter of fact, Trudeau took issue with the theorists of the NDP and joined the Liberal Party, because he was attracted to the party's advocacy of an open federalism. (FFC, p.xix) For while Liberals were defending centralism in Ottawa, they also stood for provincial autonomy. (FFC, p.129) He advocated this strategy for socialists.

Trudeau pleaded for "greater realism and greater flexibility in the socialist approach to problems of federalism". (FFC, pp.125, 142) Socialists must be pragmatic in their radical strategy and tactics, learning from Mao Tse- tung. (FFC, pp.126, 130, 146) As long as "socialism is to seek fulfilment through parliamentary democracy, with its paraphernalia of parties and elections, there will be a constant need for the tactician as well as the theorist. And both will have to be reconciled by the strategist."(FFC, p.128)

What strategy did Trudeau advocate? "I should like to see socialists feeling free to espouse whatever political trends or to use whatever constitutional tools happen to fit each particular problem at each particular time." (FFC, p.125) Socialists "must stand for different things in different parts of Canada." (FFC, p.128) "Socialists can stand for varying degrees of socialism in various provinces of Canada by standing in autonomous provincial parties.... In building a national party of the left, consideration must be given to what is provincially possible as well as to what is nationally desirable."(FFC, p.128) According to Trudeau, social democrats have dogmatically defended centralism insisting on a nation-wide socialism first and the same sort of socialism throughout the country. Consequently, the C.C.F. made few electoral gains. (FFC, p.129)

According to Trudeau, socialists must use the existing federal system in Canada. (FFC, p.128) He viewed federalism as the means to implant "radicalism in different parts of Canada... in different fashions." (FFC, p.130) Regionalism provided a tactical means to the growth of radicalism.   (FFC, p.133) Mao's experience "might lead us to conclude that in a vast and heterogeneous country, the possibility of establishing socialist strongholds in certain regions is the very best thing." (FFC.p. 126)

Trudeau supposedly symbolized what has been labelled the end of ideology. This new politician symbolized what sociologist Daniel Bell really meant, namely, the end of liberal ideology in the fifties and the coming of radical ideologies in the sixties. As the young New Leader, Trudeau presented the foundation of a socialist ideology, a new set of values, and new economic structures based on socialist planning. (FFC,p. 150, 146)

Socialist planning of the economy by the central government and provincial governments cannot be separated from socialist political theory. "Investment planning and resource development, for instance, both become in the last analysis matters for political decision." Political decisions will be made about the "social value" of business enterprises. (FFC, p.146) Economic planning must be decided on the "political realities" at a particular time. "The true tactical position of the democratic socialist is on the left" of the liberal and conservative, "but no further." (FFC, p.128) Imposing across the board wage and price controls in 1975 was presented as something the PC Party supported (without emphasizing the strategic difference) and then telling the people that "we are attacking these problems as Liberals."

He argued that socialists like the NDP must water down their dogmatic centralism, and defend centralism through federalism rather than appearing to favour only a unitary state. They must accept federalism as a fact and as a positive tool rather than an obstacle.(FFC, pp. 124, 125) It is a "valuable tool...from which the seed of radicalism can slowly spread." (FFC, p.127) "And since the future of Canadian federalism lies clearly in the direction of co-operation, the wise socialist will turn his thoughts in that direction, keeping in mind the importance of establishing buffer zones of joint sovereignty and co-operative zones of joint administration between the two levels of government." (FFC, p.141) In short, socialists should not be dogmatic about federalism or its particular form, not rigid, but flexible in their approach to federalism as a means to the goal of social radicalism throughout Canada.

The question of centralization or decentralization cannot be answered abstractly and absolutely in a Constitution. According to Trudeau, the Canadian nation can move towards centralization or decentralization. (FFC, p.125) Predominance of provincial or central government depends on the "economic and social circumstances, external pressures, and the strength or cunning of various politicians." (FFC, pp.37-38) It also depends "upon the immediate needs of the people and the temper of their various politicians. (For it must not be forgotten that these latter have a vested interest in strengthening that level of government at which they operate.)" (FFC,p.134) It also depends on the limits of human capacity for central planning. Other political scientists have taught him that " given realistic limits on human planning capacity, the decentralized system will work better than the centralized." (FFC,p.146) Thus one could work for policy planning in the central government and decentralization of administrative implementation in the provinces.

If academics, citizens, and politicians perceive that Trudeau unquestionably favoured co-operative or any type of federalism, they are deceiving themselves. If "my argument is taken to mean that the present socialist preconception in favour of centralism should permanently be replaced by a preconception in favour of provincial autonomy, I shall have completely failed to make my point." (FFC, p.125) "As a matter of fact, I might be prepared to argue that some day, if and when inter alia the political maturity of all Canadians had reached a very high level, a more centralized state would be acceptable for Canada." (FFC, p.139)

He disagreed with those socialists who take a dogmatic position on the end of federalism. (FFC, p.148) He also identified the formation of federalism as a solution to the problems encountered in the development of self-determination in the nation-state. (FFC, pp.188,192,194) It appears that he views federalism as a liberal link between tribal nationalism and progressive internationalism. Trudeau wrote that he favoured federalism, because under the historical circumstances, federalism "deliberately reduces the national consensus to the greatest common denominator between the various groups composing the nation."(FFC, p.191) At the same time he condemned "the tyranny of public opinion" because the aim of public opinion "is to reduce all action, all thought, and all feelings to a common denominator." (FFC, p.xxi) To be consistent, is then not federalism objectionable because it reduces consensus to a common denominator?

Trudeau did not believe in a classical, legal federalism, but hoped for a functional approach which would make federalism work. (FFC, p.203) A functional approach would permit him to work towards radical changes in all of Canadian society. It is possible, according to Trudeau, that "radicalism can more easily be introduced in a federal society than in a unitary one." (FFC, p.125) The beauty of classical federalism was that it constitutionally and functionally protected the diversity of human values (Catholic Quebec, socialist Saskatchewan, social credit British Columbia, and capitalist Alberta). However, Trudeau's functional approach to federalism would ultimately override the diversity of our pluralist society.

The real danger of the functional approach is that the proponents lose sight of the fundamental and constitutional differences between an open and a closed federalism. In Kiev, on his visit to Russia in May, 1971, Trudeau toasted: "Those of your countrymen now in Canada, Mr.Chairman, though many thousands of miles away from the Ukraine, find themselves living within a constitutional framework with a formal structure similar to that in the

Soviet Union. Each of our countries has chosen a federal system of government ... its very complexity is its strength, for it permits a necessary degree of flexibility.''(CC,p.202)   Ukrainians in Canada were not pleased with these remarks, but, more importantly, such functional language completely ignores the fundamental constitutional and federal differences between a free liberal democratic and democratic socialist society. There is a distinct difference between the NDP type of social democrats and "democratic socialism" which historically has led to totalitarian one-party systems. In the Soviet Union, democratic socialists such as Lenin, via promises, used federalism as a tool to spread radical socialism throughout the regions and nations of the USSR.

If Trudeau's essay on the practice and theory of federalism is taken to mean an uncritical defence of federalism rather than an effort to educate socialists in the strategy of radicalism through federalism, he will have failed to persuade the public of his point of view. In the debate over federalism, "socialists should be as detached and pragmatic as they hope to become in the debate over public versus private ownership; those are all means, and not ends, and they must be chosen according to their usefulness in each specific case." (FFC, pp.147-148)

In his 1961 essay which has been discussed in the preceding pages, Trudeau wrote that "the upshot of my entire argument...is that socialists, rather than water down...their socialism, must constantly seek ways of adapting it to a bicultural society governed under a federal constitution." (FFC, p.141)   That is precisely what Trudeau appeared to do when he joined the Liberal Party and later became Prime Minister.   The federal government's White Paper on Federalism for the Future (February, 1968) prepared by Trudeau and others is more a declaration for centralism than a defence of traditional federalism. Rather than relinquishing his own basic goals and perspectives, he is subtly converting the Liberal Party by redefining basic concepts such as liberalism and democracy. For instance, he now speaks of a liberalism of the left, and in *The Way Ahead* (1976) "sets new directions for the application of liberal philosophy...." There has been an almost absolute consistency from his early writings to his policies and actions as Prime Minister.

As Prime Minister, Trudeau has remained true to his basic priorities of the early 1960's - radical changes in Canadian society through parliamentary democracy in a federal system. Planning receives top priority in his government, and economic planning remains a matter of political decision-making as it did in the timing and manner of the wage and price controls. He has continually sought to use the controls period as a "breathing space" to develop plans for new values, new behaviours and new institutions. He continues to work with concepts such as "social value" and "social costs" in business and labour. He seeks extensive federal-provincial co-operation and consultation. In *The Way Ahead* the strategy in government planning and control of the economy is for a more general policy-oriented manner rather than the more direct intervention of the detailed controls program. There is a move towards greater centralization in planning and priorities in general cultural and economic policies as, for example, in federal control over radio and television; and more decentralization in the administrative and service areas of government (Veterans Administration to P.E.I.). Major changes in labour-management relations will be gradually introduced in the move towards industrial democracy. Trudeau has been pragmatic on the means, but dogmatic on the goals for a radically new society.

Saskatchewan Premier Allan Blakeney warned (January 1977) that if the Supreme Court of Canada rules against the province's oil royalty surcharge legislation, the Court will have assumed a new role in rewriting the BNA Act in favour of centralism and it will constitute a defeat for federalism. What can be expected from a Court which is headed by Chief Justice Bora Laskin, who was appointed by Prime Minister Trudeau? At the 1965 opening of Saskatchewan's law school Laskin "criticized the timidity of the federal government in not introducing legislation that the provinces might oppose on constitutional grounds." In a 1967 issue of *The Canadian Bar Review* Laskin wrote: " I find it difficult to believe that our federal system can endure unless Ottawa is accepted as a source of national power and authority exercisable in respect of and for all citizens of Canada." 2) It becomes very difficult to safeguard fundamental freedoms of persons and provinces if judges share the Prime Minister's functional view of federalism and law.

In his response to the Prime Minister's national address (November 24, 1976), NDP leader Ed Broadbent remarked that Trudeau's "own rigid, centralized form" was responsible for Quebeckers' rejection of federalism. However, Trudeau has never been rigid on federalism, but he has been inflexible on his radical sort of socialism. That is why he has consistently considered national socialists of the NDP and PQ variety as political reactionaries, guilty of dogmatism and tribalism. Rather than a dismal failure, Trudeau's strategy of radicalism through federalism has been a dramatic success.

A New Constitution

Canadian socialists should be as detached and pragmatic about the BNA Act as they ought to be about federalism, according to Trudeau. In the same essay he said: "A sound rule for Canadian socialists would be to insist that, if need be, they are prepared to carry out their ideals under the present constitution ." (FFC, p.149) "No longer must our federal constitution be regarded as something to be undone, the result of a costly historical error which is only retained at all because of the 'backward areas' of Canada." (FFC, pp.127, 9-10)

He told the same story to the Constitution Committee of the Quebec Legislative Committee in 1965. The Constitution can be accepted as a "datum", a matter of "fact", because the federal system is rapidly evolving into a welfare state without the slightest change in the constitution. (FFC, pp.37, 39) He condemned as "irresponsible those people who wish our nation to invest undetermined amounts of money, time, and energy in a constitutional adventure that they have been unable to define precisely...." (FFC, p.37) On March 26, 1966, he told the Quebec Liberal Party that he could "only see as incongruous and premature the pre-occupation in certain quarters with constitutional reforms", which, he said were "extraordinarily untimely".

As a constitutional expert and labour lawyer, Trudeau was not reluctant to touch the BNA Act, but he considered it "untimely" because he was preoccupied with other priorities. "I am not in a frantic hurry to change the constitution, simply because I am in a frantic hurry to change reality. And I refuse to give the ruling classes the chance of postponing the solving of real problems until after the constitution has been revised." (FFC,p.44) If there is going to be drastic revision of the Constitution, according to Trudeau, it will be on account of radical transformation of our industrial society, and the working classes will have a significant say in defining the new constitutional structures of power within society. (FFC, p.8)

Trudeau proposed that the "discussion be begun with

essentials: precise and limited they may be, but all the rest can follow." (FFC, p.59) He added that the "concepts of the 'essential' and the 'superfluous' will be defined ... according to each person's social philosophy." (FFC, p.25) His political and social philosophy has been well defined throughout this study. Discussing his attitude towards constitutional reform, he wrote: "With the exception of a certain number of basic principles that must be safeguarded, such as liberty and democracy, the rest ought to be adapted to the circumstances of history, to traditions, to geography, to cultures, and to civilizations." (FFC, p.6)

Initially, Trudeau was not ready to move swiftly on patriation of the BNA Act. In 1967 he wrote, "we wished to give the country time to reflect upon and to adjust to the new relationship of political, cultural, social, and economic forces that have been developing in the dawn of our second century." (FFC, p.59) But as Prime Minister, working for the transformation of values, attitudes, and structures in our industrial society, he wished to ensure that the new constitution reflect the new reality. It "implies an immense transformation of attitudes and of what I have called the social rules of the game." (FFC, p.50) The old liberal, imperialist colonial Constitution will become a radically new constitution, suitable for a progressive society. The Prime Minister in 1977 is in a hurry to patriate the Constitution "unilaterally if necessary". Some commentators consider it a diversionary tactic away from the economic confusion in the Fall of 1975 and the ministerial scandals in the winter of 1976 and the PQ victory in Quebec. Trudeau knows all about the tactics used by those who wish to divert attention away from the need for social reforms, but he is not afraid of radical reforms. (FFC,p.43) He has welcomed and worked for radical transformation of the economy. That is why his constitutional preoccupation at this time is so well-timed. By the time his new society is evolving, he wants to give it constitutional sanction, safeguarding his achievements. He is determined to reform the Constitution in terms of entrenching his accomplishments in a new constitution.

Constitutional expert, Senator Eugene Forsey, forecast that "what Trudeau is proposing would not in itself change the constitution by so much as one comma, except by adding the amendment formula."4) But this limited exception is precisely the problem. If Trudeau decides to act unilaterally and without an agreed upon amendment formula, the floodgate is wide open to radically change both Parliament, the courts and the whole Canadian society, including the BNA Act.

His political constitutional principles cannot safeguard representative parliamentary democracy. Rather, his basic constitutional goal is the entrenchment of values compatible with his humanistic "new society" at the expense of Parliament, a liberal democratic institution which has safeguarded political freedoms for so long.

He has viewed the Constitution as a "living" document which should be encouraged to evolve. (FFC, p.53) Trudeau has sought to place a declaration of human rights (liberty, democracy, etc.) in the Constitution in such a way as to be beyond the reach of any amendment; and another condition was "that the organization of the Supreme Court be made to depend directly on the Canadian constitution rather than solely on federal law." (FFC, p.53) He admitted that a "constitutional Bill of Rights would modify even further the concept of parliamentary sovereignty in Canada." In addition, the courts would receive much greater power under his Bill of Rights. "This will confer new and very important responsibilities on the courts, because it will be up to the courts to interpret the Bill of Rights, to decide how much scope should be given to the protected rights and to what extent the power of government should be curtailed." (FFC, p.58)

He would make a tactical error if he were suddenly to confront the provincial premiers with a fait accompli, but he may feel that he has been patient long enough. The 1964 Fulton-Favreau formula provided for unanimous consent to safeguard the "special status" of Quebec. Trudeau, in his brief to the Constitution Committee of the Quebec Legislative Assembly, rejected this formula and recommended a "concurrent majority" proposal. About five years later his critique of the Fulton-Favreau formula and alternative suggestions became the basis of the Victoria Charter which he as Prime Minister adroitly steered towards acceptance by the provinces. 5) However, majority rule, or consent from a province is only a "convention", a tradition of "practical value". (AP, p.88) He can and will, if necessary, move unilaterally by act of Parliament. This should at least require a two-thirds vote. If he moves unilaterally, Parliament had better be on its toes, because once the Prime Minister has the power to reform the Constitution within his grasp, it will be easy to further transform the powers of Parliament as well as that of the provinces. The honourable MP's have been tricked by a crafty PM before as in the rules changes. If Parliament agrees to unilateral action, it opens the avenue for the Prime Minister to push through his constitutional declaration of human rights, which in turn will severely restrict the rights and powers of parliamentary democracy. Powers would be transferred to the courts.(FFC,p.57)

On January 21, 1977 in a letter to the provincial premiers, the Prime Minister reiterated his determination to patriate the constitution, to "bring to an end this remnant of our colonial condition of a century ago." Last year, Premier Bourassa insisted on a prior agreement on the amending procedure to protect Quebec's priorities. Quebec feared that if it agreed on procedures first and left the amendment procedures for later, it might discover that its substantial constitutional freedoms or demands might be annulled. Newly elected Premier Levesque appears not to be in a frantic hurry to patriate the constitution for the same reason as Trudeau was in 1965, namely, he is in a frantic hurry to change the reality of Quebec. Although he favours changing the constitution, Levesque is more concerned about ending the remnant of Quebec's colonial condition within Canada. Thus the stage is set for Trudeau's threat of unilateral parliamentary action. Some Premiers may panic and go along with the Prime Minister. The Maritime Premiers, who strongly sided with Bourassa last year, are now ready to support the Prime Minister's position. In the absence of provincial agreement, the Prime Minister most likely will propose legislation through Parliament.

Trudeau is a superb strategist and knows exactly when and how to move in pursuit of his goals and priorities. His statement in 1967 that he "wished to give the country time to reflect upon and adjust to the new relationship of political, cultural, social, and economic forces that have been developing..." (FFC, p.59) concretely describes his concept of leadership democracy where the people are instructed, consulted, and educated to accept the new society before it is entrenched in a new constitution.

A New Declaration of Human Rights

Prime Minister Trudeau believes that every structure in Canada can be changed from Parliament to the BNA Act. (FFC, p.6) "To my mind, neither Canada's present constitution, nor the country itself represents an eternal, unchangeable reality."(FFC, p.37)   On this assumption, he has sought a restructuring of Canadian society from its values to its institutions. He has consistently sought to entrench his social philosophy of human rights in a Canadian constitution.

Language rights are basic to national unity, but, according to Trudeau, are very limited by the BNA Act. The "language provisions of the British North America Act are very limited." (FFC,p.55) In 1965 he already briefed the Constitutional Committee that the Quebec Legislative Assembly did not have the constitutional right to speak for all French-speaking citizens in Canada. Approximately 17% of French-speaking citizens live outside of Quebec. He insisted on equality of French and English from "coast to coast" including cultural mass communication such as radio and television. At all levels of the federal government "the two languages must have absolute equality....Like the United States, we must move beyond 'separate but equal' to 'complete integration'." (FFC, p.48)

Trudeau's language objectives enable one to understand better the big disillusionment with bilingualism. Like Justice J.T. Thorson, Trudeau does not stand for a "dual French-English Canada" and "equal partnership between two founding races." They do not want to go back into history, such as to a dual-nationality association under the 1840 Act of Union. For Trudeau, race and nationality are not the universal values for the foundation of human rights of language or culture. Thorson wrote: "When Mr.Trudeau expressed his rejection of the two-nation concept of Canada in favour of a one-nation concept he stated that the one-nation that he had in mind was a nation of two languages. He has never defined what he meant by this statement. He could not have meant a one-nation consisting of persons who spoke both French and English. He knows that the Canadian nation is not such a nation. Moreover, Canada will never be such a nation." 6) Like Thorson, Trudeau wants a single Canada. Unlike Thorson's traditional liberal-conservative principle that "all Canadians stand on the footing of equality with one another"7), Trudeau moved beyond this "separate but equal" mentality to a radical equality of "complete integration. " (FFC,p.48) To be more precise, Trudeau has consistently desired a "one-nation consisting of persons who spoke both French and English." In 1967 he wrote: "The right to learn and to use either of the two official languages should be recognized." (FFC, p.56) As Prime Minister he has been applying that principle. He envisions a new Anglo-Franco society. Trudeau knows that Canada is not yet such a nation, and Thorson may be right that

"Canada will never be such a nation," but Trudeau believes in bold experiments, such as his bilingualism program. Ironically, Trudeau's linguistic uniformity seems to imply more a "melting pot" mentality rather than a truly pluralistic and polyethnic country which he claimed to favour. (FFC, p.177)

Trudeau has never been content merely to extend just any level of French language. Neither has he been content with the Old French in Quebec. It has been his intention to extend progressive politics and culture through a progressive French language both in Quebec and Canada. (FFC, p.34) "For language is at once the extension of the individual personality and an indispensible tool of social organization," according to Trudeau's charter of human rights.8) Language is a tool to speak freely, but also to think progressively. Thorson correctly discerned that the enforcement of Prime Minister Trudeau's Official Languages Act "will result in discord and dissension. Indeed, it may fairly be deduced from his actions that the advancement of national unity was not his primary purpose in causing the Act to be enacted. His real purpose was due to his particular and major concern for advancing the position of French Canadians in the scheme of Confederation." 9) Thorson may be right for the wrong reason. Trudeau has not been bringing all kinds of French-Canadians to high-level positions in Ottawa, certainly not separatists or nationalists, but progressive French-Canadians, *Cite Libre* type, such as Pierre Juneau who can help socialize Canadian culture through federal means.(CRTC) Many Canadians thought Trudeau's language policy would advance national unity, but the separatist movement considers that policy quite irrelevant to their aspirations.

According to Thorson, Trudeau's lingual-cultural policy will "certainly constitute the greatest threat to the possibility that Canada will be a kind of country that its people have been trying to build and want it to be."10) At the present time it is Trudeau's turn to build the kind of society he envisions. His will and radical ideas are officially embodied in law, while Justice Thorson could not even obtain a citizen's hearing before the high court for "separate but equal" rights.

Any citizen who respectfully differs with Trudeau's vision and version of bilingualism is, in his colourful language, a "bigot", a "racist". In September 1976, he warned the media: " I hope that it would be the business of the media not to encourage that sort of thing " - that is, openline calls expressing dissatisfaction such as in

P.E.I. — which the Prime Minister considered "racist remarks of bigots and know-nothings." Of late, Cabinet ministers have been characterizing concerned Canadians, who oppose government policies, as "the lunatic fringe" and "extremists". These same Cabinet ministers hope to pass a bill to outlaw "hate" literature. Perhaps that law should be left for another government which is able to display genuine tolerance and an appreciation for freedom of speech.

In the 1976 Throne Speech there was a tactical shift of emphasis of bilingualism from the bureaucracy to the schools, but Trudeau's radical policy still stands. The latest tactic of removing the word "culture" from the proposal for patriation in order to seek agreement is just that: a tactic. It in no way changes the basic objective of achieving a progressive language as a tool for cultural objectives. The question is not bilingual rights, which are already in the BNA Act. The question is what kind of language policy: Trudeau's radical integration or the traditional pluralism of two "separate, but equal" French and English communities? It is more than a difference of means. It is a fundamental concept relating to which Canada will be built. Canada was a model of cultural pluralism. Existing inequalities, of which there were many, could have been met by giving special status to Quebec. Trudeau's confrontation and policy of complete integration has ignored the desires of Quebec and antagonized countless English-speaking Canadians.

The social and economic objectives of human rights legislation may be mentioned separately, but are integrated in his "social philosophy". From his social philosophy he approaches his economic objectives. As with language rights, he has consistently believed in absolute equality in the economic realm, the economic integration of business and labour in the transformation of industrial society.

Canadian governments have long recognized the liberal right of workers to organize and strike. Trudeau wants to strike at the individual businessman's liberal right of ownership and decision-making. He envisions the abolition of the so-called authoritarian business organization and hopes to restructure it into an industrial democracy. The "goal is not the mere inclusion of certain clauses in a Bill of Rights", as is the case in the Canadian Bill of Rights, but complete economic equality. "The erroneous, liberal idea of property helped to emancipate the bourgeoisie but is now hampering the march towards economic democracy." 11)

In Trudeau's "new society", business will not be an authoritarian institution, but a democratic institution like labour. There will be integration of decision-making; in short, economic democracy in an industrial society - industrial democracy. There will be distribution of wealth according to the standard of social justice, according to the workers' contribution to society. Equal distribution of wealth is one of the social objectives. His social-economic philosophy was already present in his perspective on the Asbestos strike.(AS, pp.336-339) In 1968 he stated that the guarantee of such economic rights is desirable. The United Nations prepared two separate covenants, one covering political (civil) rights and another on economic, social and cultural rights, because it realized the difficulty of implementing the idea of economic equality in modified, free market countries like the U.S.A. and Canada. Trudeau also suggested "that it is advisable not to attempt to include economic rights in the constitutional bill of rights at this time." 12) But the time is now ripe. A new constitution is necessary to embody the ideals of economic democracy. There are implications if approval is given. According to Walter S. Tarnopolsky, the covenant is "an instrument which, when signed by Canada and ratified by Parliament, would impose obligations not only of implementation, but also of submission to a certain amount of international supervision." 13)

Not only has Trudeau envisioned a covenant of economic rights, but he has also sought to limit the power and prerogatives of Parliament, and its power to protect political freedom. He has envisioned a "Bill of Rights...broader in scope...firmly entrenched constitutionally ...so designed as to limit the exercise of all government power...in favour of the Canadian citizen who would, in consequence, be better protected in the exercise of his fundamental rights and freedoms." (FFC,p.57) However admirable Trudeau's vision appears, the proposal reveals how far Trudeau wants to transform the constitutional parliamentary tradition. The Supreme Court has ruled that the 1960 parliamentary statute — the Canadian Bill of Rights — is considered part of the Constitution (although Trudeau does not seem to accept this ruling fully). This bill is in line with the constitutional tradition which champions parliamentary supremacy to safeguard political civil rights. Canadian citizens should be concerned about a written constitution which would, in the words of Trudeau, "modify even further the concept of parliamentary sovereignty in Canada."(FFC,pp.57-58)

People should be cautious about transferring power from the

Canadian Parliament to the United Nations in the light of the radical redirection of this agency, which is no longer dominated by principles of liberal internationalism but by international socialism. Liberal democracies are no longer in the majority. In addition, the United Nations has proven all too ineffective in the protection of human rights. The documentary *Who speaks for Man?* clearly demonstrates that the United Nations does not defend man, let alone protect his human rights. It does not protect or promote the human rights of communists, liberal intellectuals, minorities, and those of Christians and Jews in the Soviet Union or Eastern Europe. As External Affairs Minister, Don Jamieson told Ottawa church leaders at the end of March, 1977: "A double standard in the human rights field is an unhappy fact of international life." Canadian nationalists should remain sceptical that "international obligations are the most attractive source of protection of human rights simply because of the absence in a pure parliamentary system of any truly effective guarantees." 14) The above statement by Ivan Head, Trudeau's personal foreign policy advisor, is an insult to Canadian citizens and to the parliamentary system. It was the House of Commons, not the UN General Assembly, which censured the Soviet Union for arresting four human rights activists in mid-February, 1977.

The problem is not simply the absence of an effective UN enforcement machinery. It is also due to the absence of fundamental philosophical agreement on the (liberal or Marxist) meaning of freedom and democracy.

In this regard, it is of interest to note the statement presented by Pearson to the UN General Assembly on December 10, 1948. He warned that the Marxist views of human rights and those of a liberal democracy are as different "as a town meeting from a labour parade." 15)

Trudeau has written that his choice of what is meaningful and "essential" is derived from his "social philosophy". Except for certain "basic principles that must be safeguarded, such as liberty and democracy", the rest, that is parliamentary tradition, culture, economy, and even the country itself, can all be restructured.

What does Trudeau essentially mean by "liberty and democracy"? What is his philosophy of the dignity of the individual? Does he really mean what liberals have meant by these concepts, or are they defined from a radical perspective? Is personal freedom achieved through individual initiative, or via collective freedom? If liberal democratic rule is but a "convention" of "practical value", what theoretical value does he attribute to the idea of leadership democracy?

For a real international socialist like Lenin, freedom and democracy are really nonexistent until a liberal parliamentary body of bourgeoisie oppressors (nobodies) has ceased to function in a meaningful way. For Trudeau, democracy does not really exist until there is democracy in both the political and the economic sphere. "The liberal idea of property helped to emancipate the bourgeoisie but it is now hampering the march towards economic democracy." Both Lenin and Trudeau have singled out the concepts of equality, freedom, and democracy as basic. Trudeau may wish to safeguard these basic rights, but he appears to have redefined them beyond liberalism.

Trudeau's commitment to human rights would be far more convincing if he were to demonstrate his concern abroad. As a defender of the dignity of the individual, did he consider it his "regional" responsibility to protest the plight and mistreatment of Cuban communist poet Heberto Padilla on his January 1976 trip to Cuba? Padilla, who on the occasion of Castro's rise to power in 1959 wrote that "the just and human time is coming", has recently become a "non-person" and placed in solitary confinement for hinting that Castro is a dictator. Did the Prime Minister express "shame and anger" as did other international liberals and socialist intellectuals in Europe and America? Or did he exercise "excellent self-control" on this critical, international, human question?

During the first week of January, 1977 Trudeau announced his anticipated top level meeting in Moscow. The announcement coincided with Russian dissenter Vladimir Bukovsky's plea to Western leaders to put pressure on Soviet leaders to free Russian intellectuals. Will the Prime Minister defend human rights at this meeting, or will he plead non-intervention in internal affairs of a friendly country, possibly for the sake of trade and detente with the U.S.S.R.?

Rather than handing our human rights' protection over to an obviously ineffective international machinery, Canadians should uphold the traditional role of Parliament via the Canadian Bill of Rights. Under Trudeau's version, these powers would be taken from Parliament and given to the courts. Donald Smiley has remained "unconvinced that the Canadian courts are a sufficient repository of superior wisdom and statesmanship to entrust with the new functions." 16) The Supreme Court's 1976 ruling on the constitutionality of the "emergency and good government" legislation of wage and price controls might give a clue as to the protection of the rights of economic freedom. In addition, Smiley quoted from Trudeau's 1969 document, *The Constitution and the People of Canada* which read: "A constitutional guarantee of human rights would thus represent a commitment by all governments to the people - a commitment that, whatever their legislative powers, they will not deny the fundamental values which make life meaningful for Canadians." 17)   This idea is "repugnant" to Smiley. "If there is one value in Canadian life which I cherish it is that no one has yet prescribed any set of values to which I am required to assent. I hope that all citizens of perverse and independent spirit will unite to put down the arrogance of politicians who would inflict this kind of creedal Canadianism - or un-Canadian creedalism - upon us."18) Trudeau's creed is not Canadianism, not even Pan-Canadianism, but he has presented a socialist ideology (FFC, p.150) and a creedal democratic socialism in his writings.

Trudeau stated that federalism "is by its very essence a compromise and a pact ... the terms of that compromise cannot be changed unilaterally. That is not to say that the terms are fixed forever; but only that in changing them, every effort must be made not to destroy the consensus on which the federated nation rests." (FFC, p.191) However, in 1976 he destroyed that consensus when he threatened to move "unilaterally" on the BNA Act. His threat forced Bourassa into an election which resulted with a victory for the separatists. He is willing to compromise if the agreement moves in a progressive direction. Yet it is not so much Western nationalism, Quebec separatism, but Trudeau's internationalism which has placed the country on a collision course. He has pushed through "social integration" because he does not think in terms of "special status". For him, the concept of "nation" and "state" are historically "obsolete" and he is, therefore, insensitive to the nationality feelings in Quebec and rejects the "two-nation" concept as "dangerous in theory and groundless in fact." (FFC, p.31)

The radical and rigid approach of Trudeau to basic issues in Canada has resulted in greater caution by the provincial premiers on federalism and patriation of the BNA Act, and it has contributed to the move towards independence of Quebec. As Levesque said a decade ago, he is all for human rights, "but Quebec could never respect human rights voted by Trudeau...you don't respect that deeply something that is not yours in that field." 19)

Trudeau's objective to overcome parliamentary sovereignty is one thing. There is also a danger when one tampers with the common law tradition. From a functional view of law, trial by jury may be disfunctional when dealing with the "high volume-offences". But trial by jury is a basic Canadian civil right. The proposal (which was leaked to the press) to limit this basic right is, according to the Ontario Criminal Lawyers Association, "totalitarian in character and is precisely the sort of legislation that millions of our citizens immigrated to Canada to escape." 20) The editorial added: "No changes can be made in the name of efficiency which could not be made in the name of justice."

The same is true for the new immigration and population legislation. It may be progressive, but not necessarily more just. Social economic and ethnic groups warned (January 19, 1977) that the proposed bill is "a very serious threat to immigrant rights and possibly those of all citizens." Under the proposed legislation, immigrants and Canadian citizens may be required to get an exit visa. This is precisely the kind of legislation millions of citizens sought to escape in moving to Canada. However, the government has not discriminated between immigrants and citizens when it comes to mobilizing the population in order to decentralize government services and increase equality among regions. The Trudeau government has given it priority and, thus, fulfills another policy promised in the 1964 *Cite Libre* Manifesto for Canada. Radical equality via distribution of wealth and jobs takes precedent over, or at least limits, the individual's freedom to live where he desires.

Smiley wrote, that in Trudeau's *Canadian Charter of Human Rights*, "there is a pretentious...summary of the whole of the western tradition in politics....Nowhere is the elementary analytical distinction made between natural and positive law." 21) "Rights" cannot be guaranteed via a constitution or by the courts if the bases for justice in society (transcendental norms) are tossed aside as "obsolete" in favour of man's rationality. The Constitution of the U.S.S.R. enumerates and guarantees human rights, but in that country run by a totalitarian party elite, the will of the politicians is law - might is right, because law and justice have been divorced from their divine roots, natural law, and from their historical foundation.

For a society to remain just and free, it must be grounded in the absolute truth of transcendental justice.

Changing the country's Constitution is a challenging experiment. Even though Trudeau is a constitutional expert, the people should be most reluctant to entrust this power and responsibility to him for the simple yet serious reason that he looks upon law in a functional positivist way. He denies the dynamics of divine and natural law as the foundation of the nation. In addition, patriation of the BNA Act should be entrusted to leaders who attach a lasting value to the country itself, if not eternal vigilance over its liberal parliamentary democracy.

Notes

1. Michael Oliver, ed., **Social Purpose for Canada,** p. vii.
2. **Canadian News Facts,** Vol. 7, No. 23, p. 1125.
3. Pierre Elliott Trudeau, "Le realisme constitutionel," in Fox, ed., **op. cit.,** pp. 85, 87.
4. **The Financial Post,** March 27, 1976, p. 7.
5. The Victoria Charter required the approval of Ontario, Quebec, and at least two Maritime provinces and at least two Western provinces (one to be B.C.) for the purpose of amending the B.N.A. Act.
6. J.T. Thorson, **Wanted: A Single Canada,** p. 119.
7. **Ibid.,** pp. 7. 149.
8. Quoted in Peacock, **op. cit.,** p. 208.
9. Thorson, **op. cit.,** pp. 143-144.
10. **Ibid.,** p. 145.
11. Pierre Elliott Trudeau, "Economic Rights," **McGill Law Journal,** Vol. 8, No. 2, 1961, p. 125.
12. Trudeau, "A Canadian Charter of Human Rights, " in Fox, ed., **op. cit.,** p. 484.
13. Walter S. Tarnopolsky, "The Impact of UN Achievement on Canadian Laws and Practices," in Allan Gotlieb, ed., **Human Rights, Federalism, and Minorities,** p. 62.
14. Ivan L. Head, "Regional Developments Respecting Human Rights: The Implications for Canada," in Allan Gotlieb, ed., **op. cit.,** p. 233.
15. L.B. Pearson, "Human Rights," Robert A. Mackay, ed., **Canadian Foreign Policy 1945-1954,** p. 164.
16. Donald Smiley, "The Case Against the Canadian Charter of Human Rights," in Fox, ed., **op. cit.,** p. 490.
17. **Ibid.,** p. 494.
18. **Ibid.**
19. Quoted in Sullivan, **op. cit.,** p. 243.
20. Quoted in **The Globe and Mail,** September 11, 1976, p. 6.
21. Smiley, "The Case Against..." in Fox, ed., **op. cit.,** p. 493.

"The time has come ... to scrap the thousand
past prejudices that clutter up the present
and to start building for the new man."
Trudeau, 1950

"Industrial democracy ... must be reached....
It is the minds of men which must be changed
and their philosophies. Economic reform is
impossible so long as legislators, lawyers,
and business men cling to economic concepts
which were conceived for another age."
Trudeau, 1961

"The truth is that we are living in a new
economic era. It is time we faced that truth
It is time we decided how to live with it ...
The control period will ... give us the
necessary time to reform our economic
institutions, our attitudes and public policies."
Trudeau, 1976

Chapter V
A New Economic Order

Old Ideas and New Myths

Trudeau's consistency is no more apparent than in his economics. There have been no changes in his basic goals since his education in economics. He came home to test his teachers' ideas in the field of economics and politics. During the Asbestos strike he practiced his radical economics. He never wanted the labour unions to work within a mixed free market economy. As economist and legal scholar he stated his ideal of industrial democracy again in 1956 and 1960. In his *Approaches to Politics* (1958) he stated his democratic theory of confrontation. By practicing the politics of confrontation, he has confused the NDP, confused and radicalized the trade unions, brought about chaotic economic conditions, and has seen the realization of many of his radical ideas in Canada within three decades.

While (neo-) Keynesian economists have been pre-occupied with unemployment and tended to ignore or dismiss inflation, radical economists like Trudeau have pointed to the modified free market system - cyclical capitalism - as the root cause of inflation.

Concentration on inflation and the fear of inflation can create a psychological expectation of rising inflation and a climate for strong leadership. On December 22, 1969, Trudeau said that inflation was our "worst enemy". Consequently, he gave greater attention to inflation than to unemployment. Seven years later we face the same story: pre-occupation with inflation while the NDP in 1970 and 1977 emphasized great unemployment, the worst since 1958. On February 9, 1970, Trudeau called for an end to inflation by saying: "even if people do manage to protect their standard of living from the rise in prices, their struggle to do so keeps the country in a continual state of social tension and unrest.... We have no alternative. To end the injustices and turmoil caused by inflation, we must end inflation.... Inflation must be brought under control now.... This is a test for all Canada and Canadians which we must not, and which we will not, fail." "Unfortunately," wrote Peter Thomson, who quoted this speech,"the message was uttered on Feb.9,1970, when government spending for the year was $13.6 billion. This year (1975) it is estimated at $31.3 billion and rising."1) A year later, the Auditor-General, James J. Macdonell, in his 1976 report, stated that the government "has lost, or is losing, effective control of the public purse." In January 1977 we are told that the country's national debt is greater than that of Great Britain. Maxwell Henderson, former Auditor-General, told a Fanshawe College audience, according to *The London Free Press*, April 8, 1977 that federal spending has increased to " the astronomical figure of $45.1 billion, a 460 percent increase in just 10 years. " He added that Canada's deficit this year is " an astronomical and frightening figure for a country as small as Canada. " Henderson attributed the " reckless and irresponsible " spending to expedient electioneering purposes rather than on principle, such as permitting massive unemployment as a rationale for planning a new economic order.

If inflation was, in fact, our "worst enemy", why did Trudeau not act decisively, immediately in 1969? In his words, "ultimately the decisions are political rather than economic." (FFC, p.146) Economic controls are imposed and disposed of for political reasons at the right political time. Already in the Spring of 1972 he announced that a group of civil servants was studying "contingency planning for the imposition of controls" . However, controls may halt inflation "only if solidly backed by strong public opinion and strong government."2) But the political time and public opinion was not yet ripe for the new economic era. In the meantime, the economy deteriorated, undermining the value of the dollar, contributing to the psychology of inflation, consumer discontent, and demands for inflated wage and price increases. Such a development created dissatisfaction with the mixed economy -"we haven't been able to make (it) work". As a result, public opinion was readied for a call to alter radically the whole economic structure. As Schumpeter wrote three decades ago: "The first thing which must be done is to bring about inflation....Inflation is in itself an excellent means of smoothing certain transitional difficulties ... because money becomes valueless before long...inflation would powerfully ram such blocks of private business as may have to be left standing for the moment. For, as Lenin has pointed out, nothing disorganizes like inflation: 'in order to destroy bourgeois society, you must debauch its money'."3) Immediately after the PQ victory the Canadian dollar went down to 96 cents, but the Trudeau dollar has gone below 69 cents in purchasing value since the last election. The consumer price index went from 96.5 in 1970 to 142.8 in October 1975.

During the 1974 election, Trudeau campaigned against controls, because they would not work, according to him. Neither was he going to be pushed into them by the "tyranny" of public opinion or positions of opposition parties. He was going to move when he was ready with his controls plan, and ready to replenish his image and fulfill his leadership democracy. He waited until the political situation developed in the latter half of 1975: the resignation of his Finance Minister, the upcoming Liberal Policy convention, the worsening of the postal strike, public demands for him to do something about the economy, and the forthcoming by-elections in New Brunswick and Quebec, where his friend Pierre Juneau ran for Pelletier's seat. He made his famous wage and price controls speech on Thanksgiving Day, the night before the two by-elections. The opposition parties were troubled enough to lodge a complaint with the CBC which, contrary to policy, broadcast the speech just before the elections. Trudeau was very upset when Quebec politicians in 1956 practiced a similar tactic. "To have broadcast such a statement seems to me inopportune and ill-timed — I would call it immoral, if it were not for the somewhat restricted meaning that the adjective has acquired among us."(AP,p.45) But is it also not scandalous to campaign against controls, only to institute them a year later for people to obey for three years? Is that not a somewhat restricted meaning of morality in elections?

The politics of crisis provides a leader and people with a sense of crisis and challenge for strong leadership. In the name of "emergency" and "good" government, Trudeau gave his Thanksgiving Day legislation. The Supreme Court ruled it constitutional.

According to Chief Justice Bora Laskin, the Anti-Inflation Act was necessary " to meet a situation of economic crisis imperiling the well-being of Canada as a whole and requiring Parliament's stern intervention. ''4)

Trudeau had no moral right and no political mandate to move towards the creation of a new society. The opposition parties voted against the controls program and Parliament has had no initial input in the current plans for the establishment of industrial democracy.

Confrontation and Corporatism

Trudeau's course of action angered labour leaders and the NDP. Even in intellectual circles, Trudeau's radical idea was confused with corporatism. Political economist J.T. McLeod of the University of Toronto articulated that corporatism has deep roots in Canada and that "Trudeau has not invented, but merely accentuated" corporatism. But he wrote: "Paradoxically, and to his credit, one of the first opponents of such corporatism was a young man named Trudeau. In the introduction of his 1965 book *The Asbestos Strike*, Trudeau seemed more interested in denouncing the nationalist tendencies of corporatism than its economic implications."5) To his credit, Trudeau denounced corporatism, however not on nationalist, but on economic and radically political grounds. He rejected or set corporatism aside, because the social sciences "have certainly not yet shown how a legal superstructure, which makes no essential changes in capitalist institutions, could reconcile the opposed interests of capital and labour...."(AS,p.25) Most of our thinkers "regarded it as a means to tame the democratic thrust of the trade union movement."(AS,p.25)6)

Trudeau's conception of the new society is not corporatism. Unlike the Catholic and nationalist socialist, he has searched "for an approach to social issues in tune with the course of history." (AS, pp. 25,382) Historically,he did not and cannot go back to a pre-industrial, hierarchical, organic view of society. The present capitalist stage of industrialization with its unequal relations between business and labour and the insolvable problems, must be superseded by a new higher stage of industrialism (AS, pp.56, 339) where there is industrial equality, where the value of people would be judged by their contribution to society and not by what they may own.7)

The President of the Canadian Labour Congress, Joe Morris, has stated several times that the CLC "will never support a wage control program.'' Trudeau's policies, he said, ''are nothing more or less than 20th century Machiavellianism''. He considered the controls program authoritarian, inequitable, a trend towards the corporate state, and a threat to the free trade movement.8) In March 1976 labour marched on Parliament Hill and held a Day of Protest in October 1976. Labour representatives withdrew from the Economic Council of Canada and the Canada Labour Relations Council.

Like the labour unions, the NDP had campaigned against wage and price controls, only to be decimated in the election. However, in their *Viewsletter*, John K. Galbraith told the NDP to support controls, learning to distinguish between belief in permanent and NDP objections to specific provisions in Trudeau's program. The problem with the American wage and price controls program, according to Galbraith, was ''that the topside policy was set by people who didn't believe in them...the presumption that they were temporary.''9)

However, Trudeau also believed that they were temporary, not a permanent solution. The permanent solution lay beyond controls, beyond the mixed economy of the liberal welfare state. Herein lay the difference between Trudeau and former Finance Minister John Turner and his deputy minister Simon Riesman. In 1974-1975, Turner did not stand in the way of wage and price controls, but he stood in the way of Trudeau's economic plans. Like Turner, Trudeau saw controls as temporary and would agree with Turner that they do not constitute an economic policy. Trudeau would agree with the free enterprise economists from Vancouver's Fraser Institute which published *The Illusion of Wage and Price Control* in early 1976. Like the above economists, Trudeau is under no illusion about the unfairness and inequity of controls and what temporary controls can or cannot accomplish. Controls, he told a *Financial Post*-sponsored conference in October 1976, create ''their own kind of economic disruption and social injustice.'' But there is a fundamental difference in direction and determination.

John Turner believed in the mixed economy, the modified free market economy in which government has a social responsibility for welfare and in which business is responsible for economic welfare, sharing in the social-economic costs of unemployment, retirement pensions, etc., in short, MacKenzie King social welfare liberalism. Government will stimulate the free market, attempting to balance inflation off against unemployment – tinkering within the mixed economy. Wage and price guidelines or controls   would be initiated if necessary, but only as temporary measures to restore the sanity, rationality of the mixed economy. Basically, it would be a (neo-) Keynesian economics within a capitalist system.10)

In sharp contrast, Trudeau has desired the temporary controls period to transform the modified free economy into a planned economy, and restructure behaviours and values for a new society. He stated his real reforms for the twin problems of cyclical capitalism in 1956 and 1961. (AS, pp. 31-32; FFC, pp. 145-146) In his January 19, 1976 speech, he said that, "we haven't been able to make even a modified free market system work in Canada to prevent the kinds of problems we are now experiencing....The control period will not only help us to reduce the rate of inflation, but will also give us the necessary time to reform our economic institutions, our attitudes and public policies." Trudeau planned to deal with the root causes of inflation and unemployment, as he saw it. To end inflation will require a radical restructuring of human behaviour, for he believed, "that the habits that we've acquired, the behaviours that we've acquired in this two or three hundred years of an industrial society have led to sending the system out of joint."11) On the CBC program "Sunday Magazine", January 25, 1976, the Prime Minister said that thirty years of experience with the mixed economy "seems never to be able to cure unemployment completely without causing inflationary spurts.... Each successive wave brings in a greater difficulty: higher unemployment with higher inflation."

Rather than restoring or maintaining the mixed free economy, the controls period allowed a "breathing space" in which to prepare for a radically new planned economy. Therefore, Turner stood in the way. And after the absolute majority in the 1974 election, Turner became disposable. Occasionally, Trudeau would bypass Turner and directly communicate with the Deputy Minister of Finance, Thomas K. Shoyama, an acknowledged socialist and formerly chief economic advisor to the socialist government in Saskatchewan.12) Turner came to realize what Eric Kierans experienced earlier, namely, that major economic policy is not really debated in Cabinet. This lack of Cabinet participation is similar to Schumpeter's model which separated politicians from the scene of major economic decisions, which should be under the control of a central planning committee or board. The political alliance between "Mr. Liberal" and Trudeau paralleled Lenin's "formal political alliance" with the economist Pyotr Struve, "the political leader of bourgeois liberalism". At the same time,

Lenin was carrying on "incessantly a most merciless ideological and political struggle against bourgeois liberalism and against the slightest manifestation of its influence in the working class movement."13)

Riesman worried about too much Galbraithian influence in the controls period. But he need not have worried. Trudeau is neither a Keynesian liberal nor a Galbraithian economist. Trudeau has never had a failure of nerve to discuss directly the shortcomings in Keynesian economics. (FFC, pp. 77, 78, 143) As far as Galbraith was concerned, Trudeau replied in an interview: "I'm inclined to say, 'Who's Galbraith?' I have read two or three books by him. I've met him a couple of times socially. I find he is a delightful writer and thinker. But in terms of economics, you know, I spent two years studying with Schumpeter and two years studying with Leontief and if you want to know who is permeating my economic thinking you'd be better to think in terms of Leontief and Schumpeter."14) Wassily Leontief's 1938 article on "The Significance of Marxian Economics for Present Day Economic Theory" may have given his gifted student an appreciation for Marx's realistic, empirical critique of the basic structural characteristics and problems with cyclical capitalism.15) In general, people have not given Trudeau enough credit as an economist. One must have excellent economic credentials in order to be invited to attend a World Economic Conference (Moscow, 1952).

Keynes may provide the pragmatic economics of wage and price guidelines. Galbraith may be the philosopher of wage and price controls, but Leontief and Schumpeter are the Marxian economists who advocate priorities and planning of a socialist economy. In the words of Schumpeter, "Every socialist wishes to revolutionize society from the economic angle and all the blessings he expects are to come through a change in economic institutions."16) Through his radical economics and federalism, Trudeau has envisioned not only a new Canada, but a new man and a new society. In *The Way Ahead* (October 1976) the Trudeau government envisioned an inflation-free society. (p.16)

Economic or Participatory Democracy

Trudeau envisioned not only an inflation-free society, but ultimately a strike-free economy. The panacea is industrial democracy. Freedom and democracy, according to him, do not really exist until there is economic democracy.

The liberal right to strike as an economic means of collective bargaining can also be used as a means of political confrontation for radical change. In 1949 Trudeau sought to radicalize the union workers and leaders to the point where they would settle for nothing less than social radicalism, a radical restructuring of industrial relations based on equality of labour and management rather than an authoritarian business structure.

At a time of double-digit inflation, strikes may have an additional purpose: inflating an economic conflict into a political confrontation. Although he announced his across-the-board anti-inflation controls in October 1975, the Prime Minister permitted the Postmaster General to exempt the striking postal workers. The union leaders did not initially permit the postal workers to vote on the government offers. The Postmaster General, Bryce Mackasey, even warned the public against the radical political objectives of some postal union leaders. In reference to Quebec, the most strike-ridden province in the public service sector, Gerard Dion, Professor of Industrial Relations at Laval University, cautioned a Montreal audience (March 16, 1976): "The hidden objective of the common front is to destroy our economic and social system and replace it with another of Marxist inspiration." 17) With a 10-12 per cent inflation, lengthy strikes and demands for a 30-60 per cent wage and salary increase may not make sense economically, but politically they provided a province like Quebec with a PQ government committed to social democracy and a federal government with a rationalization to abandon a modified free market system.

Out of desperation, the public and small businesses which faced possible bankruptcy demanded that the government finally do something. The economic-political strike against the government (the employer) provided Trudeau with the political timing to impose his contingency plans for a new society. If the 1949 Asbestos strike signified the start of a new economic era in Quebec, the 1975 postal strike was significant, because, to use Trudeau's earlier words, "it occurred at a time when we were witnessing the passing of a world, precisely at a moment when our social framework — the worm-eaten remnants of a bygone age [inadequate ideologies and out-dated institutions] — were ready to come apart. It is the date, rather than the place or the particular industry that is decisive."(AS,p.67)

Trudeau had been living out of the new economic truth since student days. It was about time that labour leaders, businessmen and legislators also were liberated from age-old myths and live with reality, as he saw it. The Prime Minister encouraged the Postmaster General to invite labour unions to fight with, not against, the government for social democracy in a just society. Mackasey said (November 24, 1975) in Ottawa: "collective bargaining served the unions and the country well until the mid-1960's." The "adversary system" suited the past, but in the present, the "plain truth" is that the unions are "fighting against society", against the government as "our major service employer". Mackasey continued: "The unions should be fighting for a more democratic workplace. Unionists are social democrats. Their goals—at least, until now—have been worker welfare and social justice. Their stake in freedom is as big as, or bigger than, anyone's. For if social democracy dies, so do unions. Their survival, it seems to me, should impel them out of the dead end of power and back into the main road of social justice." In his (December 1975) CTV interview, Trudeau discussed economic democracy in connection with the postal strike. "If we understand and believe in what I'm talking about there will be less strikes because we will agree more in advance on what a reasonable share of the pie is, and we'd be looking at different institutions in order to try to arrive....at other means to make sure the postal workers have a fair wage than the strike method, because a strike against the government is a strike against the people...."

If the unions cannot be won over to the controls program, Trudeau told a press conference in Edmundston, N.B. (September 1976), "maybe I'll have to try bludgeoning them now." Rather than taking such dramatic steps, Trudeau has proclaimed the gospel of industrial peace through participatory democracy. The 1976 Throne Speech and pamphlet, *The Way Ahead* were full of references to peaceful and a more cooperative mechanism of industrial democracy. Since September 1976, Labour Minister John Munro has been preaching the gospel of industrial peace, and that participatory democracy is the panacea to industrial strife. He envied the economic democracies in Western Europe. He wanted business to drop its suspicion, and "invite the labour movement in from the cold," he told a Halifax forum of business students (January 20, 1977). But before labour is taken in, it had better beware of a possible government freeze on free labour unions. Why would a government which is in favour of decentralization in certain areas, favour so much greater centralization of labour organizations and business associations? Why the misgivings about independent and autonomous labour unions in Canada?

There is also a misleading implication that participatory democracy will mean less adversary industrial relations. It all depends on what philosophy underlies participatory democracy. Participatory democracy in the university may intensify rather than resolve internal relations. Demands for radical equality can create distrust between students and teachers and destroy the administration of a liberal university.

The government disclosed in the 1976 Throne Speech that it was using its various departments and crown corporations to "test new methods of improving working conditions and labour-management relations." The government has implemented them in Air Canada, Statistics Canada, Treasury Department, and the Post Offices.

Labour unions began to see the light. The 1976 CLC's "Labour Manifesto for Canada" called for, among other things, an equal partnership with business and government for "co-determination" in industrial relations. At its annual convention, President Morris was so thoughtful and successful that he was able to eliminate the negative word "social corporatism" to read "social democracy". Still, Trudeau's confrontation with labour over controls has radicalized the labour movement. Donald Montgomery, CLC Secretary Treasure told delegates to the annual meeting of the P.E.I. Federation of Labour: "The labour movement of this country has been compelled to reorient its thinking and direction from being primarily an economic organization to one of political movement." 18) The CLC was already a political movement, directly supporting the NDP.

In reality, the labour movement has been compelled to reorient its political and economic thinking radically, thanks to the Trudeau government. Dennis McDermot, Canadian Director of United Auto Workers warned the NDP that it no longer could count automatically on labor union support. It was interpreted as a warning to provincial and federal NDP leaders, but it also opened the way ahead for Trudeau in his bid to win over organized labour to his ideal of industrial democracy. Trudeau has always worked for a radicalized labour movement. Perhaps he has persuaded them in the "belief that they should take a more and more active part in politics...." (AS, p. 343) Labour Minister Munro is working hard to woo organized labour away from the NDP, flattering them with the idea that they are a force for national unity, inviting them to participate in Trudeau's idea of economic democracy. The NDP may be hard pressed to keep labour on their side, unless they switch from opposition to controls to support for Trudeau's industrial democracy. In 1970 Ed Broadbent could still write: "The Trudeau government has neither the intellectual flexibility nor the political will to institute either complete or compulsory constraints." Also, that "the central structure and the entailed power relations of our economic system remain neither equal nor just."19)

Trudeau, of course, has both the will and the determination to restructure society towards industrial democracy. And if he were to succeed, industrial relations between business and labour may be on a much more equal footing. Like labour leaders, the NDP leadership is also shifting strategy, in the direction of Trudeau's promises of economic democracy. Broadbent still calls for an immediate end to the anti-inflation program, but on the CTV program, Question Period (January 16, 1977) he was open to a "social contract approach" as in Sweden and West Germany, something on which the government is working.

Besides winning over labour, Trudeau is working on a strategy to win over business. Unlike labour, the business community supported the controls program initially. It was not the first time in history that businessmen supported strong economic measures by a political leader in the mistaken assumption that he was going to save rather than fundamentally alter the system. Now that the capitalists begin to grasp the significance of Trudeau's thoughts on the new economic order, they turn around, saying that controls must go. Health Minister Marc Lalonde attacked the "knee-jerk reaction" of business and labour at an anti-inflation seminar in Montreal. "The equally unthinking reactions by some businessmen suggests that intellectual rigor mortis is not confined to either side of the union-business fence."20)

To win over the business world to his post-control society, Trudeau has distinguished between big business and small business. In the 1976 Throne Speech, the government attached a "very high value" to small business — a "mainstay of employment". Small business was described as the "lifeblood" of most Canadian communities in *The Way Ahead* . The Task Force on Business Government Interface foresaw no fundamental problems in small business-government relations.21) Big business posed a greater problem. To bolster the government's international politics — the so-called Third Option — of relations with Common Market and Communist countries, the government wants big business to do business with communist governments and Japanese businesses. But big business is not biting. They prefer to export to the readily available markets on the North American continent. In October 1976 The Canadian Export Association released some statistics of big business which support the above desire. The McLaren Report's principal recommendation is the creation of a Canada Business Relations Council to meet ''the challenges, confronting both business and government, of the international trend toward increased government-to-government involvement in trade and investment.'' (p.1)

In the summer of 1976, the Canadian government signed a trade agreement with the Soviet Union. In October, External Affairs Minister Donald Jamieson told a group of Canadian businessmen that in the Soviet Union '' the state expects to deal with a state. I am not sure that Canadian businessmen had yet grasped the necessity for dealing with a state.'' To help find the right purpose to trade, he said, ''may be the most important place in which the government can help to clear away the underbrush....''22)

It is well to note that the objective of the Trudeau government is not to provide government support for exports where business wants to find markets, but more to discipline big business to back up the government's international political objectives. It is the difference between a liberal continental versus an international socialist view of business-government relations.

Trudeau's strategy to win over small business and to discipline big business is not original. In the transitional stage, Schumpeter said, leaders should work with the small businessmen and leave the farmers alone, as Trudeau did with the latter group in the wage and price controls period.23) Mao Tse-tung, in order to socialize capitalism in the New China, made a distinction between big (foreign) and small (domestic) enterprises. To reform big business, he won over the small businessman, promising assistance only to turn on them afterwards to complete the economic revolution. Mao said: '' Our present policy is to regulate capitalism, not to destroy it. '' Trudeau understood this strategy very well, for he reported from his travels: ''So Mao sought a modus vivendi that would allow him to incorporate into the new society all those whose experience and talent might be useful to the regime. A distinction was invented between the foreign capitalist and the national capitalist. The first was by definition an imperialist exploiter whom one could fleece and eject without scruple. The second could be transformed, thanks to that patient adaptability that characterizes the Chinese Revolution, into a 'reformed capitalist' ."24) The establishment of a Canada Business Relations Council is according to Trudeau, "part of the strategy, to enter the post-control society ... where our institutions will have been reformed."25) The patient adaptability of the Canadian businessman may transform him into a "reformed capitalist". If small or big business were to go along with this strategy to save the economic system, the assumptions may prove to have been in error. It is rather misleading that radical changes in society are done in the name of democracy and liberalism.

Implementation of the restructuring of government-business relations, according to the McLaren Report, is that "participatory democracy will take on additional meaning...." (p. 54) We are assured that the "primacy of Parliament" will be observed. Parliamentarians know what happened to the existing institution when the primacy of "participatory democracy" was introduced in Parliament. In the 1976 Throne Speech, the Prime Minister assured us that Parliament "will have a vital role to play". In *The Way Ahead*, as well as the Throne Speech, we were promised consultation and sharing of responsibility in finding the way. "It means that the government will place before interested Canadians its assessment of the major problems we must solve together, and its definition of the available options." Thus it is within Trudeau's "framework" of the policies and strategies that interested Canadians will be consulted. Parliament has been concerned from the start, but has been isolated and ignored. According to MP Herb Gray the secret task force did not provide for input by the elected representatives of the people on "these big plans for their future." It "does not provide in any way for the involvement in its work of Parliament."26)

After the government has written its secret task force report on "participatory democracy", labour and business groups are invited to be consulted on industrial democracy. Business and labour may be tempted to move in that direction. Adversary relations hurt the economy and parties involved. Who does not want to improve working conditions? Who wants to defend an authoritarian business organization, labour union, or government, for that matter?

However, in the new economy, "participatory democracy" will not necessarily mean more economic democracy or real participation. Economic policy and priorities will, ultimately, not be a joint endeavor of business and labour, but planned by government and left to business and labour to implement. Trudeau had opposed labour's tri-partite proposal, because it would take decision-making away from Parliament. Yet his economic "participatory democracy" takes decisions of economic policy and strategy away from both business and labour. (FFC, p. 146) His radical idea of absolute equality would mean complete equality of business and labour members on industrial boards, an idea still considered radical in socialist Sweden or Great Britain. Industrial democracy for labour may mean not only the end to strikes, but also the end to free trade unions. It is to the credit of the CLC that it recognized from the start of the AIB program the danger to economic freedom inherent in Trudeau's approach to economics. The free labour movement is "in the battle of its life," said CLC President Joe Morris in March 1976 in Ottawa. John Eleen, research director of the Ontario Federation of Labour, fears that "calls for worker control are really for control of workers."27) And these fears are not unfounded. In social democratic countries worker control may work, but in democratic socialist societies, it means control of workers.

For an opinion as to the growth of freedom or industrial democracy in a socialist-oriented society, one can turn to Schumpeter. Although socialists claim that there cannot be real democracy except under socialism, Schumpeter saw no necessary compatibility or incompatibility between socialism and democracy. He admitted that much of economic democracy (democratization of decision-making in industry, profit-sharing) "will vanish into thin air in a socialist regime." And he added: "...the task of keeping the democratic course may prove to be extremely delicate....After all, effective management of the socialist economy means dictatorship not of but over the proletariat in the factory....As a matter of practical necessity, socialist democracy may eventually turn out to be more of a sham than capitalist democracy ever was. In any case, that democracy will not mean increased personal freedom."28) Schumpeter also saw history as marching towards the inevitability of socialism, but he was enough of a realist to perceive that it will not usher in a new heaven on earth. "In particular there is little reason to believe that this socialism will mean the advent of the civilization of which orthodox socialists dream. It is much more likely to present fascist features. That would be a strange answer to Marx's prayer. But history sometimes indulges in jokes of questionable taste."29)

One rather questionable joke is that leadership democracy has been promoted in the name of liberalism and through the Liberal Party. Apparently Trudeau can say anything he wishes about liberalism. In the December 1975 CTV interview, he said he did not believe in "the absolute liberal state". He approached liberalism "not (as) a doctrine. It is not something you apply. Liberalism is a way of thinking." Massive government intervention in free institutions indicated an "advance in liberalism". His framework for *The Way Ahead* "sets new directions for the application of liberal philosophy in the light of the economic and social conditions of our time."(p.5) Rather, he has applied his old ideas to liberal institutions. He advanced liberalism to what he called "liberalism of the left" — it is really left of liberalism. Under his definitions, liberalism becomes mere Silly Putty.

His consistency and radical ideas are best illustrated with reference to the liberal and national socialist welfare state. He has not envisioned "statism" or the continuation of the welfare state. Already in 1958 he remarked that a nation which continually requests more and more handouts or welfare, becomes "a craven people that makes itself the servant of the state, and this is the true definition of totalitarianism."(AP, p.70) That is a revealing, new definition of totalitarianism. In his January 19, 1976 Ottawa speech he stated that the "size of government at all levels...cannot escape the spotlight of re-examination" and he saw "no intrinsic reason why governments should stay forever in the business of providing services which could be performed by the private sector."

The above statements do not mean that Trudeau has retreated from his desire to restructure society radically. "This government has no intentions of lessening its commitment to its fundamental social goals."30) He found a "third option" for government — a middle road between "minimal role", a conservative view, and a "continually expanding" role of the welfare state of the liberal or NDP variety. Hence, the emphasis on decentralization of the service role (health, education, etc.) to the provincial governments and "reprivation" of certain government corporations (Canadian rail roads) to the private sector. "The role of government policy should not be to direct and manage the economy in detail."31)

It has been Trudeau's desire to set the priorities and policies. He told the Ottawa audience that he viewed the role of government as a protector and promotor of the "public interest; and that therefore the legislative and regulatory aspects of government might well have to increase in the future." What is envisioned is not less, but a more efficient government commitment to social-economic objectives.32) It is basically government planning for a socialist-oriented society. As he stated in *The Way Ahead*, "these principles...could ultimately reshape the nature of government's role in our society." In brief, centralized planning of social-economic priorities and policies, and decentralization of social services.

There should be no mistaken assumption that the mixed free enterprise system will be protected. There is a desire for a planned and directed society. Already in 1961 Trudeau stated that the debate over public versus private sector is a pragmatic problem of means to serve socialist ends. (FFC, pp.147-148) Upon analysis, no ground can be found to indicate that he has retreated from his former desire to radically restructure government and society. The Throne Speech, *The Way Ahead*, and the MacLaren Report make frequent references to the market sector, to market power, but nowhere and no longer can one find references to the free market. The Throne Speech spoke about the "free play of market forces", but not of promoting the forces of the free market in a mixed economy. Addressing the conference of the Canadian Grocery Distributors' Institute, Liberal MP Robert Kaplan, parliamentary secretary to the finance minister, said that the Prime Minister and the Liberal Party have an "'Ideological commitment' to a 'freer working of the market place '", but apparently not the working of the free market.33) Like Schumpeter, Trudeau has no ideological commitment to the working of the free market. The market will be made to work for a planned economy. The welfare state, like the mixed economy, will belong to the scrapheap of history. The liberal state, like the formerly pervasive Catholic church, will be an obsolete institution, conceived for another era. Like Schumpeter said, the liberal state "will form part of the ashes" when the new socialist regime takes over.34)

In the name of applying liberalism to a new era, man and society, industry and government are radically restructured. In fact, Trudeau advanced liberalism beyond itself. Possibly, he agrees with Schumpeter when the latter wrote that people "will swallow anything provided it is served up in the garb of familiar slogans." 35)

At the Liberal Policy Workshop (March 23-26,1977) time-worn socialist ideas were sold as the "New Liberalism". Senator Maurice Lamontagne, Co-Chairman of the Conference, defined them as a "Liberal Revolution", rather than as a   revolution over liberalism. Describing the role of a prime minister who gives himself, Schumpeter stated: "He will lead party opinion creatively - shape it - and eventually rise toward a formative leadership of public opinion beyond the lines of party...." 36) Since the Asbestos days, Trudeau has tried to alert and educate public opinion to accept his government's assessment of the major problems and its definition of the available options within the given framework. He has given formidable leadership on bilingualism and federalism to the point that the Liberal party is largely non-existent in the West and almost a third party in Quebec, attracting no one group in the country. Before he became Prime Minister, Trudeau once said: "I would not hesitate to follow any policy...whether other people call it socialist, capitalist, or free enterprise or anything else" so long as it "can solve a given problem without destroying the basic beliefs which I have in man, in freedom and in democracy." 37) Immediately after Trudeau's new economic policy speech in Ottawa, conservative columnist, Dalton Camp, predicted that the "ingenious" Trudeau will campaign in the next election as the "greatest champion of Free Enterprise. " 38) Perhaps some columnists may call it Trudeau-style capitalism or the Canadian way.

Trudeau is hardly a conservative or traditional liberal, because he told the Canadian Club in Ottawa that "it will do no good to try to create a pure free market economy to solve our future problems, because that won't work either." As has been demonstrated, Trudeau has been remarkably consistent in his political philosophy and goals which he has creatively and concretely worked out under Canadian federalism. Already in 1961 he wrote: "Of course there is need for doctrinaires of a sort...who will constantly expound what they think to be the nearest thing to 'pure' socialism. For, it has been often observed, the dreamers of today [1946-1949] frequently become the realists of tomorrow [1961-1965]; and the educational value of painting utopias [1968] has repeatedly been established by the eventual realization of such goals through the democratic process [1978]. (FFC, p. 128)

However, if Trudeau has decided to bring about "fundamental change", wrote Denis Smith, editor of *The Canadian Forum* , "then he has no mandate", and "is in the wrong party." 39) The labour union-oriented NDP may not want Trudeau. During the Asbestos strike and the anti-inflation controls period, Trudeau acted as if he knew better what was good for the workers, better than the labour unions. The Liberal Party does not believe in creating a "new man" through politics, and Trudeau received no mandate from the people to create a "new society". The NDP leadership is aware of the price the Party paid for supporting Trudeau's minority government. They knew in 1969 what he meant by reform of parliamentary government.

In the name of "participatory democracy", Trudeau pulled the rug out from under the parties and Parliament. In the name of "participatory democracy" in industry, business and labour may suddenly face a completely new set of rules. The people should question more critically the Canada Trudeau has been in the process of building. Who should decide what is "good" for the people? They could be more cautious in giving up basic economic and political freedoms for a false sense of social security. Trudeau's new society is not necessarily more just and tolerant than a liberal democratic society.

Notes

1. **The Montreal Star,** November 15, 1975.
2. **Canadian News Facts,** Vol. 6, No. 12, July 4, 1972, p. 850
3. Schumpeter, **op. cit.,** pp. 226-227. On October 27, 1969, economist Eric Kierans advised the Prime Minister to adopt a floating rate to protect the Canadian dollar, but Trudeau waited until May 1970. Kierans asked Trudeau when he had last heard about a floating dollar. Trudeau "said he wasn't sure but he thought it was perhaps six months later. I said, 'No, it wasn't; it was one billion, two hundred million dollars later.'" Quoted in Stewart, **op. cit.,** p. 170.
4. **Canadian News Facts,** Vol. 10, No. 13, July 17, 1976, pp. 4-5. It was a case in which the Prime Minister needed Parliament to give the legislation legitimacy. If he did not use the parliamentary process in "emergency" legislation, it might be ruled unconstitutional as was the "order-in-council" decision of Ontario Premier William Davis. Then one must call the legislature into special session to make it legitimate retroactively. Chief Justice Laskin said that it "is beside the point" if in other periods of crisis no similar action was taken. The point is that similar action was taken in the 1970 so-called "October Crisis." The politics of crisis may constitute the norm under the politics of confrontation.

5. J.T. McLeod, "The Free Enterprise Dodo is No Phoenix," **The Canadian Forum,** August 1976, p. 12. Trudeau discussed corporatism when he dealt not with the negative nationalist leaders, but with the positive message of the social teachings of the Catholic church in Quebec. See AS, p. 382 for Trudeau's excellent definition of corporatism.

6. McLeod did not expect much from Trudeau's so-called corporatism and concluded that "socialists have a special obligation and a unique opportunity to re-formulate their primary principles and values." **Ibid.,** p. 13. Mind you, Trudeau provided such a " marxist class-struggle analysis" already in 1949 during the Asbestos strike and in the Introduction of the 1956 book on the strike. In several old and 1976 New Year speeches and interviews, he provided the nation a special challenge to re-formulate values and primary institutions, yet McLeod did not, or claimed not to, see the thrust of Trudeau's challenge.

7. CTV Interview, December 27, 1975.

8. See Joe Morris, "Towards a Corporate State," March 1976; a pamphlet published by the CLC.

9. Interview with J.K. Galbraith in **Viewsletter,** February 1976, p. 8. It is "like putting Xaviera Hollander in charge of anti-pornography," he told a Queen's University audience. (October 18, 1976)   See **The Student,** November 1976, p. 8.

10. See W.A. Wilson for an interesting summary of "Two Views of Market Economy, "**The Montreal Star,** March 17, 1976, p. 9.

11. CTV Interview, December 27, 1975. **The Toronto Star,** January 3, 1976, p 4. The Trudeau government may pride itself in reducing the rate of inflation, but the United States achieved similar objectives without extensive controls and expansive Anti-Inflation Board. In addition, inflation may be down, but unemployment is high. The unemployment rate might go down more with another liberal politics of investment and profit than with the present government's job and work programs. The economic costs of AIB are staggering, growing from a staff of 60 to 850 at a cost of about 18 million dollars. This may be minimal if and when the AIB is restructured into some sort of economic planning board.

12. See Walter Stewart, "Shoyama: A Socialist Becomes No. 2 Bureaucrat," **Maclean's,** July 1975, p. 4. Shoyama "is second highest priest of all, inferior only to Pitfield."

13. Possony ed. **op. cit.,** p. 433. Trudeau has been engaged in an ideological struggle against the bourgeois mentality in the trade union movement since the Asbestos strike. Then already he advocated against compromising within a modified capitalist society.

14. **Maclean's,** September 6, 1976, p. 19. Trudeau may have been impressed with Galbraith's emphasis on the indispensibility of the scientific and technical elite in politics (**The New Industrial State,** 1967). But unlike Galbraith who advocated a technocratic — "end of ideology" — politics, Trudeau was determined to imbue politics and science with a new humanism. (AS, p. 347)

15. Instead of building a Republic of Technology, he wanted to build a Republic of Humanity. Trudeau has also acknowledged the influence of the outstanding teacher, the British neo-Marxist Harold Laski. It is possible that Laski's radical critique of liberalism may have shaped Trudeau's approach to traditional liberalism.
16. Schumpeter, **op. cit.,** p. 169.
17. Quoted in **The Montreal Star,** March 22, 1976, p. 5.
18. Quoted in **The Montreal Star,** February 12, 1976, p. 5. See also "The Revolt of the Middle-class Worker," **Maclean's,** February 23, 1976, pp. 22-30.
19. Ed Broadbent, **The Liberal Rip-off: Trudeauism vs the Politics of Equality,** pp. 39, 76.
20. **The Telegraph Journal,** January 30, 1976, p. 17.
21. See **How to Improve Business-Government Relations in Canada** (Also referred to as the MacClaren report.) September 1976, p. 49.
22. **The Globe and Mail,** October 29,1976.
23. Schumpeter, **op. cit.,** p. 221.
24. Quoted in Schramm, **op. cit.,** p. 166, Trudeau and Hebert, **op. cit.,** p. 99
25. **The Toronto Star,** October 13, 1976, p. 8.
26. **The Financial Post,** April 10, 1976, p. 7. Peter Brimelow, Business editor of **Maclean's** was concerned that the fundamental reorientation of business and government downgraded Parliament by not including it in the fundamental debates. Brimelow believed that it was the beginning of the corporative state rather than a continuation of the principle of participatory democracy. See **Maclean's,** December 13, 1976, p. 68.
27. **The Toronto Star,** November 13, 1976, p. B4.
28. Schumpeter. **op. cit.,** pp. 300, 302.
29. **Ibid.,** p. 375.
30. **The Way Ahead,** p. 7.
31. **Ibid.,** p. 23.
32. **Ibid.,** pp. 23, 26.
33. **The Toronto Star,** February 9, 1977, p. 9
34. Schumpeter, **op. cit.,** p. 169.
35. **Ibid.,** p. 360.
36. **Ibid.,** p. 277.
37. **Canadian News Facts,** Vol. 3, No. 7, April 19, 1968, p. 50.
38. **The Telegraph Journal,** January 27, 1976.
39. Dennis Smith, "Controls and 'the New Socialism'" in **The Canadian Forum,** February 1976, p. 42.

"Some are elected to political office by defending the people against dangers that are either exaggerated or imaginary... We must stop trembling at the thought of external dangers...."

Trudeau, 1950

"We found ourselves questioning longstanding institutions and values, attitudes and activities, methods and precedents which have shaped our international outlook for many years."

Trudeau, 1968

"We are now reorienting our foreign policy, our trade policy, and indeed our military policy in a way which is breaking the pattern of the past 100 years."

Trudeau, 1974

Chapter 6
A New World Order

A Radical View and Review

Trudeau has remained consistent in his economic ideas and in his conception of the world, especially world economics. If cyclical capitalism is the cause of inflation, capitalist imperialism is one of the root causes of world wars.

As a teenager at the height of the Great Depression, he said, "I obviously didn't see any political significance at all. But when I went back after the war and saw the consequences, I began to look for causes. I found them in economic crises and in nationalism, which I have always detested." 1) During the 1968 leadership campaign, he explained, "I have been taught to keep away from imperialistic wars." 2) Possibly by Schumpeter and others, he has been taught that a root cause of world wars is economic imperialism.

With the above assumption, and since America is a great economic power, an "overpowering presence" (CC, p.159), it is no wonder that Prime Minister Trudeau immediately called for a radical review of Canadian foreign policy. Since "Canada's relations almost anywhere in the world touch in one way or another on those of its large neighbour," the United States cannot be dealt with like Europe or Latin America under a separate sector, but is discussed throughout most of the foreign policy papers. 3)

The foreign policy review was radical. In March 1969 he told the American press that Canada was concluding its "first methodical and total review of our foreign policy and our defence policy since the end of World War II. We have gone back to first principles in doing so, and we are questioning the continuing validity of many assumptions." (CC, p. 173) Five years later he told American businessmen: " We are now reorienting our foreign policy, our trade policy, and indeed our military policy in a way which is breaking the pattern of the past 100 years. "4) And, after Trudeau obtained an absolute majority in 1974, his personal foreign advisor, Ivan Head, reported that Trudeau was determined to take a new activist role on the left of international politics.

The radical redirection of foreign policy was not simply a shift from Pearsonian liberal internationalism to the pragmatism of Trudeau, as apparently Peter Dobell believed. 5) Such an interpretation failed to distinguish between pragmatic radical strategy and tactics in politics and new international values in social philosophy, between political realism (factual conditions) and new socialism in international affairs.

Trudeau's foreign policy, as his domestic policy, evolved from his "scale of values" (CC, p.154), his vision of world history, his perception of reality, shaping events and crises accordingly. He valued socialist humanism (FFC, p.150) a "more enlightened humanism", a "universalism", a new world order. 6) "The world must be our constituency." (CC, p.137) "One world is not likely to be achieved in the next decade or so", but "such a development might appear in principle to conform to the natural course of the world's evolution."7) The review document, *Foreign Policy for Canadians*, continued: "In essence, foreign policy is the product of the Government's progressive definition and pursuit of national aims and interests in the international environment. It is the extension abroad of national policies."8) Trudeau stated his policy and strategy as soon as he was elected Liberal leader. "It must be a policy which is pragmatic, realistic, and which contributes effectively both to Canada's political survival and independence and to a more secure, progressive, free and just world society." 9)

The Prime Minister has said that our foreign policy should "further Canadian interests". (CC, p.161) What kind of Canada has he envisioned? "We are building a new society in Canada. It should not be surprising that the external manifestations of this society may be somewhat different than has been the case in the past." (CC, p.173) What are the internal manifestations of this society? "Canada is a reproduction on a smaller and simpler scale" of the new universal world order which he has envisioned. 10)

    This emphasis on a universal world order, makes the traditional distinction between domestic and foreign policy historically, if not politically, obsolete. The new internationalism emphasizes the "maximum integration" of foreign and domestic goals.   11) As Ivan Head said, the objectives "are neither exclusively foreign nor exclusively domestic." 12)   Hence, economic aid is no longer "foreign aid", but development aid. In line with the above priorities, the Trudeau government established the new agency for international aid (Canadian International Development Agency, CIDA) which operated without parliamentary control. From Trudeau's world economic perspective, he considered the national aspirations in Quebec a "world tragedy", a "sin against humanity", a "crime against the history of mankind", rather than a national tragedy and a case against confederation. If Trudeau's internationalism were to secure a world society, how could he at the same time secure the survival of Canada as a nation? It is one thing to give up sovereignty, but quite another to give up national independence. As a matter of fact, Trudeau's internationalism has been jeopardizing national unity.

    The truth is that Trudeau did not provide a Canadian foreign policy, but a new foreign policy for Canadians, foreign to the history of Canada as a liberal nation. What should concern Canadians is not so much the supposed "anti-Americanism" of the policy, but the anti-liberalism of Trudeau's direction, his radical break with liberal internationalism of Canadian governments since World War II. "What was most striking" about the foreign policy review, wrote Jack L.Granastein, "was the government's evident willingness to abandon the past." 13)

    The principles which previously were the foundations of Canadian foreign policy and had guided Canada's conduct in international affairs since World War II, were set forth in the 1947 Gray Lecture by Louis St. Laurent, then Secretary of State for External Affairs. The five principles were: 1. national unity, because there is a consensus "that our external policies shall not destroy our unity"; 2. political liberty in the French and English liberal tradition, because the concept of freedom is "debased" and under attack; 3. respect for the rule of law, for the principle of natural law which "is a necessary antecedent to self-government." Without it, "lawlessness is practised in the field of international relations"; 4. a defence of human values of "a Christian civilization," of moral principles of good and evil in human relations; 5. "The acceptance of international responsibility in keeping with our conception of our role in world affairs" namely, the development of Western freedom and democracy. 14)

Trudeau's radical departure from the above liberal principles was evident from his perspective that authority and government are not founded on divine law and natural law, and political conduct does not rest on moral principles of good and evil. (AP, pp.31, 32) He has appeared to be more committed to international than to national unity. He has continually spoken of freedom and democracy, without explicitly defining the content. And, instead of accepting international leadership in keeping with a liberal Canadian conception, he apparently has imposed his radical conception of world order on Canada as an independent nation.

During the previous Liberal governments, we may have been less independent from the United States than desired, but relations were not only friendly between people, but also between governments because there was a liberal consensus on the defence of Western freedom and democracy. In this respect, it may be interesting to compare the policies of two liberal leaders: Prime Minister Trudeau and the late President John F.Kennedy. During the 1968 election, Trudeau was favourably compared to Kennedy, in charisma and intelligence. However, a fundamental difference became apparent in their respective acceptance of responsibility in world affairs.

President Kennedy's foreign policy was not a fundamental departure in purpose from the previous administrations - he offered a new strategy to meet communist objectives. Kennedy sought to end the cold war strategy (primary reliance on the negative strategy of military aid and security alliances). He replaced it with the positive economic-political strategy of development aid to challenge communists on their own grounds in the Third World. Although Kennedy was not a cold-warrior, he was a devout anti-Marxist. He seized the initiative to turn the revolutionary tide in favour of liberal democracy. The global challenge, according to Kennedy, was that liberal democracies, not communist countries, "should be marching at the head of this world-wide revolution," and we should not allow "the communists to evict us from our rightful estate at the head of this world-wide revolution." 15)

The Vietnam War was later considered not only a military mistake, but an error which led to a questioning of the American mission in the world. America lost face not only in Canada and the Third World, but students and scholars in the United States also lost faith in America as a revolutionary model. New left scholars like Richard Walton and the journalist David Halberstam concluded that America has been on the "wrong side of history" and, therefore, counter-revolutionary, and that the Vietcong were the "genuinely revolutionary force." 16) The Canadian government changed its outlook on American involvement in Vietnam, which is reflected in the foreign policy review of 1970. 17)

Trudeau, as a brilliant student of international politics and economics, had concluded twenty to thirty years earlier that history was not moving in the direction of traditional liberal democracy. His view of history was that of a "caravan of humanity" moving "towards the left".(AS,pp.339,345) He was not going to be left behind to "perish in the desert of time past". He was one of the first of the New Left intellectuals in the fifties.

Trudeau joined the caravan of world history in favour of radical change, change in the direction of social radicalism. He did not see his role as a re-actionary moral crusader against communism — he was determined to be "realistic", to be with the wave of the future. Trudeau was the first of Western leaders to face the "reality" of history. By extending the hand of genuine friendship as Prime Minister of Canada, the Trudeau government has made communism politically respectable in the world and diplomatically acceptable in the West. As Trudeau said in Caracus, January 1976, "a short time after I went to Peking, President Nixon also went to China and a short time after I went to Moscow, he went there, too."18)

In the very first issue of *Cite Libre* (1950) he criticized the Catholic church and French Canadians for blind spots, imagined external and exaggerated fears of communism. Again in 1956, he was critical of the churches' and nationalists' condemnation of communism and socialism. (AS, p.52) In 1968, he said that "we are not so much threatened by the ideologies of communism or of fascism" as by world hunger. (CC,p.154) Speaking to the American Congress (February 22, 1977) he spoke about the "rigidity in our response to" world poverty and hunger, and that our approach to peace has been "little more imaginative than was our sometimes blind grappling with absolutes in the international political sphere".

By inviting the intellectual Trudeau to Moscow (1952) and China (1960), these communist nations certainly bet on a winning horse. As Trudeau said, the Chinese are "betting on a sure thing." 19)

Trudeau signed a protocol arrangement with the Soviet Union on May 19, 1971, which placed Canadian-Russian consultation on the same basis as those with Great Britain, America, and Japan. The protocol provided for economic, scientific, and cultural co-operation, because "we have a great deal to learn from the Soviet Union... a country from which we have a great deal to benefit...."(CC,p.159) On the basis of such cultural exchanges, and economic trade, the present reality of basic differences in systems can be overcome by means of knowledge and understanding, promoting "true friendship" and common objectives of universal peace, "a world without war, a world in which governments are at the service of man". (CC, pp.151, 152) Immediately upon his return, he told the House of Commons that he wanted to achieve a "climate of confidence, a climate in which men of differing social and economic systems trust one another.... In this way... slow progress toward a world in which the foremost goals of every government of every country must be the attainment of social justice, fundamental human rights and the dignity and worth of all human beings." (CC. p.150)

One need not be opposed to hockey diplomacy or trade and aid for the Soviets with their wheat shortages. However, one should not be so naive as to accept the underlying assumption that such exchanges form a real basis for friendly relations or better understanding. It is one thing to sign a trade agreement to promote trade, but if a country signs a pact, as Russia and Canada did in the summer of 1976, it may result in a rising of false expectations and misunderstandings among Canadian business about trade with the Soviet Union. The Soviets trade for political reasons. That makes them better businessmen, driving a harder bargain than the American or Canadian businessman who may want to make a fast buck without much foresight.

The international politics of sport may be bad for both sports and politics. Canadians are treated to numerous Russian-Canadian hockey games, but both Hockey Canada President Alan Eagleson and Bobby Clarke, President of the NHL Players Association, said that the overcrowded schedule is bad for hockey sports. Are political relations set back every time the Canadians lose? Is it of educational or propaganda value when a Canadian teacher returns from the

Soviet Union and cannot understand what the language fuss in Canada is all about? Has she really understood why there is no official languages problem in Russia? Whatever value the various exchange programs may have, political problems require political solutions.

It is not only naive to assume that cultural exchanges can solve political problems. The foreign policy review is also based on the mistaken assumption of "a slow evolution toward more liberal communism, still under Soviet control however". 20) Detente demands trust and that is what Trudeau apparently has in the Russians. Increasing contact with the Soviet Union can speed up the "slow progress" towards "fundamental human rights and the dignity and worth of all human beings". (CC, p.150) Despite the Russian invasion of Czechoslovakia, Trudeau agreed to a Russian policy of peace by detente and disarmament in Europe. However, the evolution of communism has not been towards a "more liberal" communism. The de-Stalinization of Russia has led to the re-instating of a more Leninist communism, which is not more liberal. The medical mistreatment of Marxist intellectuals has taken place under the more pragmatic Leninist leaders. Even though Andrei Sahkarov said that detente has brought greater denial of human rights, and former KGB agents like Alexei Myagkov (*Inside the KGB,* 1976) warned that detente was used for espionage, the Trudeau government has been determined to pursue detente. James Eayrs asked the critical question years ago: "But what climate of confidence can exist between a totalitarian police state and a society with pretensions to openness and freedom?....Who denounces the crimes of Kosygin? The tiny band of courageous Soviet intellectuals who try are taken without trial to jail. Every day is War Measures Day in Moscow."21)

Trudeau may be depressed at times about Russia, but has been impressed with China since his student days. He has never believed in monolithic communism, and wanted to enlighten Canadians on the significance of Chinese communism, because, "China is a country on the march." 22) In 1949, as an "inquisitive and fraternal traveller", he witnessed the failure and fall of an authoritarian democracy under military tutelage in nationalist China. He downplayed the importance of his 1960 visit to China as a private citizen. He correctly said that other Canadians and leaders visited China. True, in 1960 Red China made an extra-ordinary propaganda effort to win the friendship of Third World countries. But what two other "private citizens" from

Canada received a lengthy audience with Chairman Mao and Chou-en-Lai? 23) In 1960 he travelled to China as a private citizen and met the wise old men of radical change and strategy, who represented "the triumph of an idea, an idea which has turned the entire world upside down and profoundly changed the course of history". 24)

The two travellers were not so much innocent as naive. If the authors "are guilty of anything, it is naivete...the naivete to believe that what we saw with our own eyes did exist... the further naivete to think that our readers capable of making the necessary adjustments in the often outrageous claims made by our Chinese informants. That is why we didn't always think it essential to interpose our critical judgement...." 25) They seem to have had rather high expectations of the readers' ability to make the necessary critical judgement, on the part of those who were not there. It is also somewhat ironic that Trudeau felt compelled to impose his critical judgement on an authoritarian regime in Quebec, but not on a leadership democracy like Red China (in Mao's words, "The People's Democratic Dictatorship".)

In 1960 as well as in 1968, Trudeau wrote that it "seemed to us imperative that the citizens of our democracy should know more about China." 25) But what did the private citizen, Trudeau, really know about the political and economic development of China? Is there not some ignorance in a statement that "China is already proving that it can become the leading industrial power in the world....Naturally China is still far from possessing the industrial equipment of countries that began their industrial revolution fifty or a hundred years ago"? The base for industrial development was established between 1926-1936, as shown in the study of John Chang. 27) If it had not been for the war with Japan in the 30's and 40's, and the communist experiments in the 1950's and 60's, China would have been an industrial power in the 1970's.

The trip to China was not only intellectually productive, but also proved to be politically profitable for the Chinese, The little book about Red China did not say much "about international politics, because little was said to us in China on the subject." 28)   But Trudeau knew that "Time is on its side, and China is in no hurry - except on one point: Taiwan.... The Communist Party regards Taiwan as a matter of honour.... Let us simply add that the 'two-China' policy is based on profound ignorance of the Chinese mentality." 29)

The private citizen, Trudeau, remembered all this when he became Prime Minister. One of Trudeau's first significant political decisions was to recognize Red China diplomatically. Since Trudeau understood the Chinese mentality, he has consistently referred (from the 1968 leadership race to the 1976 Summer Olympics) to the nationalist government of Taiwan, not of China. In Vineland, Ontario (March 3, 1968) he gave a guarded answer to a question concerning China by saying that "Canada could continue relations with the Chiang Kai-Shek government.... Taiwan has every right to be recognized since it has had stable government for more than twenty years...." On the occasion of the 1976 Olympics, Trudeau wanted to welcome the nationalist athletes of Taiwan, but not as representatives of China. He told the House and Olympic Committee: "We welcome the athletes from Taiwan. We hope they will compete. We do not discriminate on the basis of sex, race, or indeed, national origin...this is a one China policy...we do not let athletes come into Canada...to pretend that they represent a country, China, that they do not represent. That is all we are saying." (July 12,1976) Trudeau was saying quite a lot, practicing differentiation on the basis of international politics in a peaceful sports event. Olympic officials charged that Trudeau had changed the existing "understanding" of the rules of the game. Canadian people, newspapers, and opposition politicians accused Trudeau of capitulating to economic greed and communist pressure (selling wheat). The reaction was based on a profound ignorance of Trudeau's politics. He taught the members of the Olympic Committee a lesson in international politics: not Taiwan, but the communist athletes are the representatives of China. To underscore Trudeau's position, Marc Lalonde, Minister of Health, expressed the hope that the People's Republic of China will be part of the 1980 Olympics in Moscow. Speaking at an All-China Sports Federation reception in Montreal, Lalonde said: "I hope this indeed is the last Olympics in which we will have seen one-quarter of the people of the world not participating."30)

With respect to a China policy, there is also a profound difference between Prime Minister Trudeau's and President Nixon's trips to China. To pick up the pieces of Kennedy's strategy, Nixon proposed a "New Strategy of Peace". Seeking an "honourable" way out of Southeast Asia, Nixon, the complete pragmatist, went over to the "enemy". The radical Mao, who was not above opportunism when it came to strategy, came over to the imperialist enemy. But the

Chinese leaders distinguish between so-called friends and genuine friends. The Soviet Union used to be a genuine friend, but today there is every reason to conclude that this is no longer true. When Trudeau went to China as a private citizen in 1960, he saw the future. As Prime Minister, he built his foreign policy, and the recognition of Red China, on the basis of principle, out of a sense of progressive history.

Development and Defence

From the fundamental difference in views of world history flows a fundamental difference in foreign and defence policy. There was a shift of emphasis from peace-keeping or security to peace-making, the building of peace through development aid to the Third World. If the cause of world tension is believed to be economic rather than ideological, one could expect a greater priority on economic growth than on a strong defence system. Consequently, Trudeau has given greater priority to planned economic growth and development aid than to national and international security. In this respect, there is also a fundamental difference in defence policy between Kennedy and Trudeau.

Rather than defending the existing political-economic order, the Prime Minister has championed the building of a "new international economic order". He has perceived world conflict not in terms of communism versus liberalism, but between the rich and the poor nations. Therefore, one must work for a redistribution of wealth among nations. At the University of Alberta (May 13, 1968) he said: "Unless Canadians are aware of the vital goal our aid is seeking to achieve, they may not be sympathetic to a change of this sort....In order to be effective it will...be costly. Yet we and the other developed nations have no alternative. The world can not continue to accommodate mutually exclusive blocs of rich nations and poor nations. We must recognize that, in the long run, the overwhelming threat to Canada will not come from foreign investments, or foreign ideologies, or even - with good fortune, foreign nuclear weapons. It will come instead from the two thirds of the peoples of the world who are steadily falling farther and farther behind in their search for a decent standard of living. This is the meaning of the revolution of rising expectations."(CC,p.139)

There is nothing wrong, and much is right, with aiding other people in the world, with helping develop their economies and nation-state. But it is Trudeau's political perception of the world and his socialist sense of economic guilt and responsibility which requires closer analysis. In his major speech in Ottawa (1976) on the new economic order, he spoke of the "unique opportunity to make a major contribution to social justice and political stability in the Third World.... How long can our consciences ignore the suffering of other human beings? How long will a hungry world tolerate the unthinking and habitual waste of limited food resources? How long can we close our eyes to the international responsibilities imposed upon us by our wealth and others' needs?" In the Throne Speech of 1976, Trudeau again returned to development aid and the task of "shaping a new international economic order". The point is not only that Trudeau neglected to acknowledge the enlightened contributions to foreign aid by the previous Liberal governments, but wanted to make a case for a planned international economic order, at home and abroad. How rational is the foundation for most "development aid"?

British economist, P.T. Bauer, an expert in international economics has written a critical analysis of the rationale behind most development aid programs to the Third World. By reference to the facts, he empirically refuted the preconceived Marxist notions of imperialism by Western democracies. He proved several basic assumptions to be totally false. For example, he disproved the beliefs that prosperity is achieved at the expense of the less well-off; that incomes are "extracted"; that poverty can be attributed to colonialism; and he showed that the term "economic colonialism" is a distortion of the truth. 31) Such erroneous views of reality lead to erroneous views of the people of the Third World, as for example in attitudes of condescension and contempt towards the rich plurality and potential among these different people and nations). Such distortions of reality have been primarily promoted by workers in international organizations and by people in the West; "some...see the Third World as a useful instrument for promoting their cause in what is in essence a civil conflict in the West." 32)   A new international economic order will most likely be shaped by these same people who have been able to unite the extremely diverse elements of the Third World only by concentrating on "enmity to the West" which happens to be politically and economically profitable for these nations. 33) How just will the "new order" be if nurtured on enmity?

The relationship between rich and poor nations requires a solution, and we must carry our full responsibility in feeding the hungry. However, socialist intellectuals have turned the problem into a principle of world history. From their vision of an international class struggle, they have elevated the problem into the principal issue of world politics: a struggle between the "haves" and the "have nots", the "blocs of rich and poor nations." (CC, pp.137, 139) Therefore, the world is not threatened by "the ideologies of communism", but by "two third of the world's population - that goes to bed hungry every night." (CC, p.154) One reason why one third of the world does not have enough to eat may be caused by the "ideology of communism", the forced collectivization in China and Russia. At one time the Ukraine was the breadbasket of Europe. Today the free Ukrainian farmers in Canada supply much wheat for Russia and China.

How many countries, which give economic aid, show equal concern about the discriminatory and oppressive practices of the governments receiving aid? For example, the Prime Minister has protested the military use of peaceful nuclear material in India, but did he express a genuine concern about the curtailment of human rights (civil and political)? Although Bauer presented a well-reasoned statement on the problem, he did not expect to have much influence. "Argument and evidence will not affect conduct and measures which are rooted in emotion, often reinforced by the play of personal and political interests." 34)

In   the Kennedy model, modernization was to combat communism positively, an "historical demonstration" of the superiority of the liberal democratic model of revolutionary change. For Trudeau, history demonstrated that the world was moving towards the left. Rather than combatting communism, his strategy was designed to build a new international socialist-oriented world. This difference in world perspective has obvious consequences for a nation's defence policy. While Kennedy emphasized development aid, he did not neglect national and international security. The political security and defence of a modified free economy depend upon military security and defence of national sovereignty. President Kennedy wanted to be armed "beyond doubt". His strategy of modernization was backed up by "strategic bombing". Rostow, who helped devise this strategy considered economic growth, political order, and (inter-)national security the "three abiding tasks of government." 35) Trudeau may have been impressed by Rostow's earlier edition (FFC, p.127), but Trudeau has elevated the strategy of Economic Growth to the fundamental principle of peace. 36)

The low priority of (inter-)national security in Trudeau's review of foreign and defence policy caused great consternation in Canada among political and military leaders. According to Bruce Thordarson, former Prime Minister Pearson, a Noble Peace recipient, emphatically rejected Trudeau's choice of economic growth as the highest priority. 37) Trudeau's priority was based on his view of reality, namely, that there was no communist threat. Fearing no aggression, he pursued a positive policy of true friendship with communist countries. Only a week after the invasion of Czechoslovakia, when most liberals were still in a state of shock, he showed little concern and "reiterated his view that detente was possible if all parties displayed a desire for it." 38)   Apparently armed invasion was irrelevant as long as one expressed a verbal desire in detente. There is "one fact that tends to allay our fears: China is historically more an 'aggressed'than an aggressor nation." 39) The Russians historically claim the same reality; consequently they demand "national security" via almost totalitarian control over Eastern Europe. Perhaps neutralization of Western Europe will be sufficient. But since they also fear American aggression, they have been actively seeking friendship with Canada.

From the above knowledge and understanding of reality, Trudeau has proceeded with the political decision regarding Canada's role in NATO. (CC, p.167) Politically, there are indications that Trudeau was personally committed to complete military withdrawal from NATO. His personal advisor, Ivan Head, had prepared a secret report which was delivered only hours before the Cabinet met to discuss NATO. Neither External Affairs Minister, Mitchell Sharp, nor the Minister of National Defence, Leo Cadieux, knew anything about the existence of the secret report. As Pearsonian Liberals, they put their principles and policy down, insisting that Canada remain in NATO. A "right compromise" was reached, that is, a compromise in the right ideological direction. The fundamental military step had been taken - away from NATO. 40)

The decision on NATO reflected Trudeau's radical strategy of pragmatic compromise on tactics, but his insistence on maintaining the overall left-of-liberal objectives. Most internal support came from Marchand and Pelletier. Trudeau's objective was pursued with a minimal military commitment, but concentrated on transforming NATO from a defence institution against Russia into a political institution of detente, thus indirectly supporting the Soviet's long-range strategy of neutralization of all of Europe. The only known external influence on Trudeau's thinking about NATO in terms of detente was the "intellectual socialist" Pietro Nenni, the Italian Minister of Foreign Affairs. 41) In spite of the fact that Trudeau was in favour of detente and arms reduction by both Canada and the U.S.S.R., he moved unilaterally and refused to seize the opportunity to achieve mutual arms reduction. In addition, this went directly contrary to the prevailing NATO policy. 42)

It is most ironic that the call for a strong military force in the free West has recently been coming from communists outside of Russia, even from China. The Prime Minister told a Queen's University student body (November 8, 1968) that from his "scale of values", "in a very real sense we are not so much threatened by the ideologies of communism or of fascism....I am perhaps less worried now about what might happen over the Berlin Wall than what might happen in Chicago, New York, and perhaps our own great cities in Canada." (CC,p.154) Kennedy saw the struggle over Berlin as part of a greater struggle over the free world.

Trudeau did not want to isolate himself completely from Europe, only to minimize European defence. Socialist and communist members of European parliaments also pursued a strategy of political detente. Yet Trudeau wanted the best of both worlds: trade with Europe, but not the corresponding aid to military defence which will ultimately make trade possible across the Atlantic. Let us assume for a moment that his withdrawal from Europe was to meet domestic requirements. A decade after his new defence policy, the Canadian armed forces are still not equipped to defend national sovereignty.

Reality shows a Soviet presence which looms large in the Atlantic and along the Canadian coast, but Canada is in no position to protect even its own territorial integrity and fishing grounds, especially since the 200 miles zone. On August 5, 1976, a Soviet reconnaissance plane crashed off the Newfoundland coast. NATO nations had a keen interest in knowing the purpose of the plane and its sophisticated equipment, but Russian, not Canadian, ships were first on the scene to pick up the debris. An additional factor is mentioned in a report in *Maclean's*. "The Canadian military might have also been expected to capitalize on the latest evidence of regular Russian spy flights along the fringes of Canadian airspace by beating the drum for a well-equipped and active Canadian coastal defence. Yet this has not happened. The reason: Canada's relations with the

USSR are generally good, and Ottawa did not want to create troubled diplomatic waters just before the late August visit to Vancouver by three Soviet Warships. " 43)

In his new relation with the Soviet Union, Trudeau has spoken about the realization "that we are geographically continuous." From this "top-of-the-world perspective" Canada has friends to the North. (CC, p.144) But when he addressed the House regarding a new defence policy he still spoke in terms of the old geography. "The good fortune of geography has removed Canadian territory from physical contact with wars elsewhere; the good fortune of history has given us land frontiers with only a single, friendly nation." (CC, p. 157)

For years the government has maintained that coastal patrols were adequate to meet domestic defence requirements. But it took the loss of Dutch seamen in 1976 before the Ministry of Defence admitted that surveillance was not adequate. Canada's defence has been equipped neither to meet its national needs nor its international obligations. In January 1977, the Conference of Defence Association passed a resolution stating: "Defence equipment and stores are insufficient to meet our national and international commitments and contingency requirements." 44)

The Defence Department can no longer ignore the Soviet threat to the coast and seas off Canada. Ironically, Trudeau has urged Canadians to be understanding of the Russians. Speaking at the CDA convention, Defence Minister B. Danson, said that the Soviets "are determined that no future war will be fought on Russion soil." Soviet strategies in Europe account for more than mere self-defence. Instead of trying to rationalize away Soviet intentions, the responsible military and intelligence leaders would like to understand what Canada's rational defence policy is in the face of the overpowering presence of Soviet sea power.

If the Prime Minister does not want to listen to the repeated warnings about the Soviet Union from York University professor, John Gellner, an expert on the now almost extinct Naval power, 45) perhaps the warnings of Alexander Solzhenitsyn will carry more weight. He is a Russian intellectual who has figuratively risen from the depths of human deprivation in Russian prisons. "I'd like to make myself clear: the situation at the moment is such that the Soviet Union's economy is on such a war footing....The West is on the verge of a collapse created by its own hands.... Nuclear war is not even necessary to the Soviet Union. You can be taken simply with bare hands...Now it is the Soviet Union that has the navy, controls the seas, and has the bases. You may call this detente if you like, but after Angola I just can't understand how one's tongue can utter the word." 46) Both Solzhenitsyn and Trudeau agree on the importance of morality in world politics, but are worlds apart in their moral orientation. Besides ideological differences, there is also the practical difference, a difference between merely visiting the Soviet Union and experiencing the totalitarian system. Solzhenitsyn said: "My warnings, the warnings of others, Sakharov's very grave warning directly from the Soviet Union, these warnings go unheeded. Most of them fall, as it were, on the ears of the deaf. People do not want to hear them. Once I used to hope that experience of life could be handed on, nation to nation, and from one peron to another. But now I'm beginning to have doubts about this. Perhaps everyone is fated to live through every experience himself in order to understand."47)

However, the Canadian people were not given the opportunity to formulate their own opinions, because the CBC refused to broadcast the prophetic message of Solzhenitsyn. Who knows what might have happened! After the BBC showed the interview, Lord George Brown, former British foreign secretary was so moved by the message that he quit the governing Labour Party, because it refused to give freedom to individuals. The announcement caused consternation in the Party, as Labour was about to fight a crucial by-election. 48) Imagine, if it had been shown on CBC and several Cabinet members and Liberal MP's responsible for external affairs had experienced similar "conversions" and caused a corresponding consternation! In the opinion of Robert Nielson, "The CBC found two hours of prime time recently to broadcast a two-year old import, Hearts and Minds - a totally unbalanced blatantly anti-American documentary on Vietnam. Watching it, one might suppose that North Vietnam had won the war without killing anyone or destroying anything. Like most of the Western media, the CBC does its bit to sustain the big lie that the United States is the prime villain in world affairs, the chief disturber of the peace."49)

Kennedy is now portrayed as a counter-révolutionary, a warmonger rather than a peacemaker. In principle, however, he saw the world conflict with communism as a confrontation between freedom and coercion, democracy and dictatorship, between "different meanings to the same words — war, peace, democracy, and popular will." The contest in the world is a "battle for minds and souls as well as lives and territory. And in that contest, we cannot stand aside." 50) In this contest, Canada appears to have stood aside as Trudeau joined the "caravan of humanity" as it moved left.

Rather than applying liberal policy to the new international realities, Trudeau has applied old socialist ideas to the seventies. There are striking similarities between the assumptions underlying the government's foreign policy review and the socialist foreign policy views advocated by Kenneth McNaught, especially with respect to the implications about American militarism, imperialism, and the origins of the Cold War. 51) The radical foreign policy review of the Trudeau government appears to rest on a revision of the origins of the Cold War, which was popularized by the New Left historians in the sixties. Even though the Cold War may be dead, barriers still remain. As long as there is no completely free and open interaction of people and ideas across all borders, the West is well advised to maintain an effective and rational defence for national and international requirements.

The foreign policy review is an interesting example of decision-making by means of participatory democracy. On May 29, 1968, the Prime Minister announced the decision to re-evaluate thoroughly Canada's foreign policy, and announced crucial decisions which had already been made (recognition of Red China, high priority to assistance of Third World countries, more contacts with French-speaking nations, and greater contact with nations not traditionally close to Canada). From his references to new realities in the world, including the situation in Europe, it could be deduced that Canada's role in NATO was in for a change. "We shall take a hard look at our military role in NATO...."

At the outset of the NATO review, Trudeau stated his desire to gather advice "from all possible sources." Views and reports were gathered from several areas. 1. Academic Views. 2. The Parliamentary Committee Report. 3. Special Task Force on Relations with Europe (STAFFEUR) 4. External-Defence Report. 5. Trudeau and Ivan Head. 52) Numerous contacts were made by Trudeau and his ministers with the academic community. The views of academics ranged from continued military commitment in NATO to complete withdrawal. The final government decision did not reflect either view, and, therefore, satisfied few academics.

The Parliamentary Committee held hearings at which a number of witnesses presented various positions similar to those of the academics, but also a basic continuation of current policy with adjustments as deemed necessary. The members appeared receptive to a more moderate approach which emphasized NORAD. During the fact-finding tour of Europe, they received persuasive arguments for Canada's continued participation in NATO, including the military. There was general agreement among the members that Canadian forces should remain in NATO and the final report conveyed this message. They suggested that changes could be made in 1972 when certain equipment became obsolete. "The final recommendation was an uncontroversial statement that Canada should in future emphasize the political functions of NATO and encourage it to seek detente and balanced force reductions with the Warsaw Pact countries." 53) The influence of the Parliamentary Committee Report on the government position appeared minimal, according to Thordarson. At most, he thought that their recommendation may have had some moderating influence in the Liberal caucus.

One of the civil service reports was by the Special Task Force in Relations with Europe (STAFFEUR). This interdepartmental group studied the Canadian relations with Europe, covering defence, political and economic areas. "As for NATO, the Task Force concluded that Canada should continue to station troops in Europe since it was in Canada's economic and political, as well as military, interests to be actively involved on the continent." 54) This report was rejected by the Cabinet.

The External-Defence Report analyzed the more limited area of Canadian military equipment and international obligations. Concerning NATO, it presented a list of options, while more or less favouring the status quo. The Cabinet also rejected this report, due in part to the failure of the report to analyze thoroughly the effectiveness of the military capability of the system.

All of the above reports failed to coincide with the Prime Minister's perspective and philosophy. Therefore, he requested a secret report to be prepared under the direction of Ivan Head - neither the Minister of National Defence nor the Secretary of State for External Affairs was consulted. It was this report which became the guiding philosophy and policy for the government. Trudeau may have compromised somewhat in the face of strong opposition within the Cabinet, but the direction of Canada's role in NATO had been decided. In retrospect, the entire policy review process was merely a search for an acceptable rationale for the direction which Trudeau had already taken in his speech of May 29, 1968. This becomes abundantly clear from the fact that, after official committees held months of hearings and investigations and prepared recommendations, Trudeau decided that he could only get the type of report he wanted from one of his closest advisors, Head.

Canadian-Continental Relations

Trudeau has always had in mind a strategy of social radicalism for "the whole North-American continent." (FFC, pp.131,211) His close advisor, Head, thought that "other links will in due course also develop and contribute to a climate of confidence extending from the Hindu Kush up over the Pole and down to the Gulf of Mexico." 55) Trudeau's 1976 Latin America trip to Cuba, Mexico, and Venezuela underscored the importance of his desire to strengthen the links between these progressive nations and encourage the establishment of a new international economic order.

For many years the question had been debated as to why it has been so difficult for socialism to get a foothold in North America. After thirty years of academic reflection on the socialist success in Saskatchewan and failure in America, sociologist Seymour M. Lipset realized that it could not be merely attributed to a difference of cultures. He has concluded that the predominence of liberalism on the continent accounts for the failure of radicalism. 56) Fifteen years ago Trudeau taught socialists that it was just as difficult to establish radicalism in Quebec or the West, as it was on the whole continent. A separate Quebec "will not change the rules and the facts of history, nor the real power relationships in North America." (FFC, p.211) Historically, America and Canada may not be rooted in feudalism, but from a radical perspective, they are deeply rooted in imperialism - therefore, the entire continent deserves to be uprooted. 57)

Canadian-American relations have been in transition since Trudeau assumed the Liberal leadership. His political attitude towards America was established well before the energy crisis and foreign policy review. The radical review was necessary on account of his world vision, his view of reality. It was ironic, therefore, that he should have been welcomed in the American capitol and Congress (February 1977) as the Great Stabilizer of the American continent, the Unifier of Canada, and a defender of Canadian capitalism. It was an important speech from a major platform, but did not herald in a new era of consensus in Canadian-American relations. Conferences, conventions, panels and publications in both countries are in vogue, but the indentification of the problems, let alone peaceful solutions, will not be found if we continue to conduct the dialogue in traditional and familiar vocabulary. Future relations must be discussed in terms of Trudeau's philosophy, politics and policies. The politics of confrontation may confuse citizens in both countries, but the way ahead is likely to be one more of tension than of trust.

Trudeau is not anti-American, but anti-imperialist - an important distinction which must be made. He is neither a nationalist in philosophy nor anti-American in policy. He is not for Canadianism, not even Pan-Canadianism.(FFC.pp.37,196) He is an internationalist; consequently, in trade and policy, he is not a continentalist, but an intercontinentalist.

His anti-imperialist attitude towards America explains the need for a "Third Option". His admiration for Castro's leadership dates at least from the early sixties. He favourably quoted the Frenchman, Michel Drancourt's recommendation: "To combat 'American imperialism', a few countries, and France in particular, would engage in a kind of enlightened 'Castroism.' " (FFC, p.14)

In 1963 he accused the Pearson Liberals of taking orders from the American "militarists". Without defending either Pearson or Kennedy, it is revealing that he used the word "militarists", which implies that foreign policy was directed by defence policy rather than vice versa, the way he correctly perceived the relation to be. (CC, p.169) At the time, American defence policy was directed by the academic foreign policy advisors who hoped to make policy rational.

The Prime Minister wants "genuine friendship with the United States" (CC, p.173), but how can one maintain "genuine" friendship with governments which may possibly risk a nuclear holocaust for the sake of national prestige 58), and fight imperialist wars in Vietnam? It all raises questions of value and concern to "live in the shadow of the United States and its foreign policy". 59) From this perspective, the U.S.A. is an "overpowering presence" and a danger to Canada "from a cultural, economic and perhaps even military point of view." (CC, p.159) Not surprisingly, Trudeau demanded a radical review of relations with the United States, and arrived at a so-called Third Option, an association with Europe and Japan, diplomatic relations with Russia and China, and an alliance with the Third World countries for a new economic order.

The politics of confrontation seizes the opportunity to explode temporary problems into a rationale for a radical review of political or economic relations. When the American government, for example, in August 1971 imposed an import surcharge which adversely affected all trading partners, only the Trudeau government made it a major issue of trust, sowing distrust among Canadians with "all these ifs". Trudeau said: "If they do realize what they are doing and if it becomes apparent that they just want us to be sellers of natural resources to them and buyers of their manufactured products - all these ifs - we will have to reassess fundamentally our relations with them, trading, political and otherwise. "60) Trudeau demonstrated no such fundamental distrust when the Soviet Union invaded Czechoslovakia in 1968. Even though it greatly disturbed other NATO countries, he went ahead unilaterally with his military withdrawal from Europe. One week after the invasion, he casually promoted detente as if nothing had happened. But is the overpowering presence of the Soviet Union in Europe and in the Americas a less frightening form of imperialism than the American presence near Canada? In inventing the "Third Option", Liberal Senator George C. van Roggen, Chairman of the Standing Senate Committee on Foreign Affairs, told a Toronto audience (November 9, 1976), "we were left with the impression that we were endeavouring to reverse history and ignore reality in order to find an alternative to our United States relationship."61)

Trudeau's interest in international socialism and a Canadian nationalism are not mutually exclusive. K.R. Minogue wrote: "Marxism and nationalism are both revolutionary doctrines, and to that extent they can co-operate in attacks upon the status quo." 62) Pierre Vandeboncoeur, founding member of the *Parti Socialiste du Quebec*, explained it as follows: "Quebec nationalism will become explicitly socialist or else it will remain impotent....There is thus a natural convergence between nationalism and socialism.... Socialism would open up vast new perspectives for nationalism; and in return nationalism would prove to be the making of socialism."63)

Trudeau, on the other hand, appears to have been afraid that nationalism could prove the unmaking of socialism, that is, international socialism. In a "colony" like Quebec, Trudeau invited the enlightened nationalists to join him in the experiment of "social radicalism".(AS, p.343) Unenlightened nationalists or socialists, like

the separatists were downgraded to reactionaries, and counter-revolutionaries. He has tried to enlighten the nationalists in the reality
and morality of "Getting it Back" from Canadian and American
businessmen.

Accordingly, both foreign control and Canadian ownership are a
problem for him. "If, for instance, it is going to remain morally wrong
for Wall Street to assume control of Canada's economy, how will it
become morally right for Bay Street to dominate Quebec's - or for that
matter - Nova Scotia's?" (FFC, pp.202, 12) Outstanding economic
nationalists like Walter Gordon and Eric Kierans never fully
understood Trudeau's patient moves to socialize rather than
nationalize Canadian business. According to Trudeau, the right
nationalizes, but the left socializes. (FFC, p.169)

In an excellent article, Abraham Rotstein described the old
"New Nationalism" without once specifically referring to Trudeau's
new internationalism. To his credit, Rotstein realized that there is
little Canadian nationalism on account of continental liberalism,
integral to Canada and America. Opposing international liberalism
"is not, in the first instance, Canadian nationalism, but a more
diffuse, unfocused and potentially very powerful force in Canadian
politics - grass-roots populism," rooted in the land (homestead) and
space (national sovereignty). 64)   He described Prime Minister
Trudeau as: "the upper-class man in populist clothing." 65) If one
recalls what Trudeau has said all these years about national
sovereignty and attachment to the land-agrarianism, even agrarian
socialism, such a description is hardly accurate.

If Rotstein still thinks in terms of reactionary concepts like
nationalism, he will not grasp the building of the new international
economic order behind the government's establishment of PetroCan.
A government oil company, wrote W.A. Wilson, political editor of
The Montreal Star, is "justified perhaps in socialist ideology but
certainly not in economic terms.... The expenditure, if it should be
made, would have only an ideological justification and not one that
most Canadians support at the polls." And he added: "Unfortunately, there is a powerful group of liberals dedicated to the
proposition that, when a government is in political trouble, its best
solution is to move to the left. They seem to have the Prime Minister's
ear."66) But if in trouble, you do not move the Liberal Party to the
left for short-run popularity — Trudeau moved it to the left out of
solidarity with the people of the world. PetroCan is not part of

Canadian nationalism, but a demonstration of his determination to build a "new international economic order". This emphasis is clearly stated in Trudeau's Ottawa speech (January 1976) and 1976 Throne Speech. It has become part of the government's activist role on the left in international politics.

To underscore Trudeau's new internationalism, he appointed the internationalist Maurice Strong as Chairman of PetroCan, which in turn took over Arcan from the private wastemakers. Unlike the new national capitalists in the Middle East (and Alberta?), the establishment of PetroCan provided an "opportunity to make a major contribution to social justice and political stability in the Third World." Trudeau has envisioned an independent and socialist-oriented Canada. The New Left way is patriation of and participation in the Canadian economy. The objective is "to increase the ownership and participation of Canadians in the Canadian economy." 67)

In cultural affairs, like economic affairs, Trudeau has not pursued a policy of anti-Americanism, but anti-imperialism. He revolted against "the mass-consumption society of North America with its lack of humanism." 68) In 1965 already, he said: "The state must use its legal powers to compel the economic community to favour certain values that would otherwise be destroyed by the pressure of economic forces... must intervene to ensure the survival of cultural values in danger of being swamped by a flood of dollars." (FFC. p.29) The "open culture" about which he spoke and which he has sought for all Canadians are values that are supposedly "international and common to all men." (FFC, p.29) But if the common man does not want them and prefers "North American" consumer values, Trudeau believes that it is within his right to impose his progressive values. He has sought to promote, not "poor" backward French, but a "progressive" language and cultural policy from coast to coast. Such a progressive culture will produce "real philosophers, real scientists, real film directors, real economists...true statesmen...."(FFC, p.34)

Aside from the desirablitity of mass-consumption, does North American society really lack humanism? Or is it in possession of a liberal humanism? It appears that Trudeau has sought to replace this humanism with historical materialism. From his *Cite Libre* article to his 1968 foreign policy review, and even in his vision for the society of 1978, Trudeau has contrasted the emphasis on quantity with his "quality of life", forgetting that a liberal society is also tolerant and that a mixed free market economy is also committed to the Good Society. The values of a liberal welfare society are not given a completely fair treatment under his critique.

Instead of promoting a Canadian culture, the Trudeau government is promoting a progressive culture in Canada through mass communication, especially radio and television. The problem of American ownership and deletion of American commercials on Canadian TV is nothing compared to the fundamental constitutional battle within Canada over control of content in communications.

The Canada he wants to build through radio and television is basically a monolithic society, rather than a country of cultural pluralism. He has consistently sought a radically integrated society in which all Canadians will equally enjoy his humanist values. It is one thing for the federal government to regulate radio and TV communication. It is quite another thing for Ottawa to work for nation-wide control of content. The semi-secret deal with the Manitoba government to give the province control over distribution facilities and the federal government responsibility over content is of far-reaching significance. It is another example of centralization of priorities and policies, promotion of a progressive society, and decentralization of administration, of distribution to the provinces or "privatization." Not surprisingly, the provincial governments of Quebec and Saskatchewan want their own control of content. Their desire is much more in harmony with Canada as a cultural pluralism than Trudeau's vision. If Trudeau should succeed, there will not be a new Canadian culture, but a new culture for Canadians.

The cultural revolution is also taking place in Canadian universities. Some academics are critical of behaviouralism in the universities and see it as a superstructure of American imperialism. There is much wrong with American behaviouralism, but its scientific roots are in European thought. There is also the mistaken criticism that American behaviouralism promotes a separation of the disciplines. However, like the so-called "Canadian approach", one of the outstanding features of the behavioural approach is that it emphasizes "an integrated social science". 69)

Although one can understand the decision of the Ministry of Manpower and Immigration to restrict immigration of foreign academics, from the "practical" problem of manpower, it raises serious questions of academic freedom. At stake is the freedom of universities to appoint faculty members, and the potential governmentalization of the universities. Perhaps Trudeau's warnings about industry are applicable to universities. "It is always costly and inefficient to choose men or to favour institutions on the basis of their ethnic origin rather than their particular aptitude or competence." Great universities, like "great industries cannot promote maximum efficiency by ethnocentric policies, any more than by nepotism." (FFC, p.24) The Prime Minister knows all about this from his own experience when an ethnocentric Quebec government prevented the highly competent Trudeau from obtaining a university position. On the NBC Meet The Press program (February 27, 1977), Trudeau said that limiting "the number of U.S. professors teaching in Canada is a dangerous way to try to create a sense of national identity."

The recently released report, *To Know Ourselves* by the Association of Universities and Colleges of Canada, underscored the problem of content in education. As the Symposium in *The Canadian Forum* (June-July, 1976) indicated, the controversy centered as much around the concepts of Canadian studies as the content. The content which most academics want to put into "Canadian Studies" is derived from their scientific ideology rather than political nationality. The Symposium reflected the current critical question of which scientific ideology - radicalism or liberal social science - will control the soul of the university and determine the direction of studies in Canada. When political scientist Ph. Resnick wrote that we want action in Canada, a competent social theory "that leads to revolution" 70), he has expressed the scientific ideological sentiments which Trudeau stood for twenty years earlier. (AS, pp.37, 39) As a reflection of the pluralism in Canadian society, universities should champion academic pluralism.

Like many secular social scientists (behavioural and radical), Trudeau has separated social science from moral philosophy, turning his "real" social science against the moral, theological foundations of authority and obedience. Thus we have witnessed the radical secularization of academic and political life in Canada. It is not surprising, therefore, that the academic community has been, to a large extent, morally silent about the morality and legitimacy of certain policies of the Trudeau government.

American imperialism is a threat, but "enlightened Castroism" in Africa has apparently not profoundly affected Canadian-Cuban relations. A decade ago, with reference to Canadian intervention in

Nigeria, the Prime Minister said: "To intervene when not asked...
would be an act of stupidity...a presumptuous step, an arrogant step
for a country so distant." (CC, p.180) In his January 1976 trip to
Cuba, Trudeau cautioned Premier Castro about upsetting the balance
in Africa, but did he call it an "act of stupidity"? Castro is reported to
have replied that he was invited to provide a counter-balance against
counter-revolutionary troops from South Africa. But what about
Cuban troops fighting against the indigeneous national forces which
were fighting for their freedom? Trudeau told reporters that he
still opposed foreign intervention in Angola, but came out of his
discussions with Castro "with a much greater knowledge of the
situation as seen by Dr. Castro." He was impressed with Castro's
great knowledge of Africa and understood that Castro committed
troops in a distant civil war only after "a great deal of thought."
71) No doubt there was a great deal of thought, because in the early
sixties, at a Tricontinental Congress in Havanna, delegates from
Africa, Asia, and the Americas pledged solidarity in the wars of
liberation against American imperialism. Thus, to intervene when
asked, and with much thought, becomes an act of statesmanship. No
wonder that in his understanding of Cuban policies, Trudeau shouted
"Viva Cuba" and "Viva Fidel Castro." To underline his
understanding, the Trudeau government has given Cuba $4 million in
grants and $10 million in loans, at 3 per cent over 30 years, with
repayments starting in 1982. 72) In contrast to Trudeau, former
President Kennedy, already in 1961, criticized Castro for becoming a
counter-revolutionary, a betrayer of the Cuban revolution. In
1976 Radio Havanna announced that Premier Castro, former Prime
Minister of Cuba, was named President "with the supreme power in
the nation." In 1976 President Ford called Castro an "international
outlaw". Prime Minister Trudeau still seems to consider him an
international-in-law, calling him a great revolutionary leader of world
stature.

Trudeau cautioned Castro not to damage his revolutionary
image in a distant Africa (Angola, Uganda) and to concentrate on the
problems on the American continent. In 1948 Castro had seized a
radio station in Bogota, proclaiming a new radical democracy for
Columbia. In the early sixties, the Cubans were operating schools for
guerilla warfare in Quebec, and in 1976 they ran a school for spies. It
is one thing for the Diefenbaker government to maintain diplomatic
relations with an independent Cuba. It is quite another to maintain

genuine friendship with, and give heavy economic aid to, Communist Cuba, a colonial satellite of the Soviet Union.

A month after Trudeau's visit, Castro went to Moscow, claiming that the Soviet Union is "the firmest bulwark of world peace...an indestructable shield that puts a brake on the aggressive impetuses of imperialism against the small and weak peoples." He did not consider Maoist China, but Cuban-Russian relations as a "model of the practice of internationalism, understanding, respect and mutual confidence." With respect to the caravan of humanity, Castro proclaimed: "One cannot stop the processes of change taking place in the world." The future "fully belongs to socialism and communism." 73) Castro has pledged continued solidarity with the revolutionary forces in the Americas, even at the price of not renewing relations with the United States.

Besides Cuba's Castro, there is Jamaica's Prime Minister (Hi) Michael Manley. Like Trudeau, Manley was a student of the neo-Marxist Harold Laski. Before he met with Trudeau in October 1976, he was interviewed on CBC's "As it Happens" (October 26) and said that he had overestimated the ability of the privileged people to listen to reason on his vision to restructure Jamaican society radically. Black radicals like Stokley Carmichael, a champion of the ideals of the Tricontinental Congress, had been active in Jamaica in the sixties. Before the December 1976 election, Manley had declared an emergency, rounding up candidates from the opposition Jamaica Labour Party. Its leader, Edward Seaga, accused Manley's People's National Party of the standard socialist strategy of blaming the opposition for violence and destabilizing the country - jailing JLP candidates - thereby confusing the electorate. The election was not a contest between the PNP's socialism and JLP's capitalism. The real contest was between Seaga's social democracy and Manley's democratic socialism.

Manley denied that he was pro-Castro, saying that Jamaica was no Cuban surrogate. Manley hailed his electoral landslide as a "victory for the Third World" and declared: "The real meaning of the victory is that the Jamaican people have sensed there is another way of living - a way in which man has dignity." At the same time, he warned of "very difficult times" ahead with fewer "frills and luxuries", demanding great sacrifices from the Jamaican people.

Soon after the election, Manley told a Russian reporter that the Soviet Union, not Cuba, was the model for the Jamaican way. Thus he

kept his campaign promise that Jamaica was no Cuban surrogate. A
year earlier, however, Castro declared in Moscow that the Soviet
Union was the model for Cuban development. It really was no
surprise, therefore, to see that Cuba was providing technical and
educational assistance. One of Manley's post election decisions was
to seize banks, including Canadian subsidiaries - while the Canadian
government was considering Jamaican development aid of $100
million.

Within Canada, confrontation between the federal government
and those of the provinces can overflow to other territories. In 1968
Trudeau told a Queen's University student audience that if in the
future there would be the start of riots and civil war in America, "I
am quite certain they would overflow the borders and they would
perhaps link up with the ... underprivileged Canadian." (CC, p.154)
However, the great riots in the American cities were not led by civil
rights leaders, but by black leaders like H. Rap Brown, Eldridge
Cleaver, and Stokley Carmichael, who thought in terms of class
consciousness, fighting international wars of liberation within the
Americas.

In Canada, it may not be so much the underprivileged
proletariat or non-violent Indians, as the overprivileged, the radical
"young, and the trade unions... the new elites in the North American
society" (CC, p.153) who may cause disturbances, disorders, and
divisions. It was the young Trudeau who sought to radicalize the
trade unions. It is the best and the brightest in Quebec who want to
divide Canada. Radical economist Mel Watkins served as economic
missionary to the Indian Brotherhood from 1974 to 1976, advising the
federal government to let the Dene Nation live. The Dene Declaration
reads like a PQ document, or an NDP Manifesto, not a native Indian
document. According to Doug Cuthand, editor of *The Saskatchewan
Indian*, elitist journalists like Marci McDonald have elevated AIM
militants to the "level of freedom fighters or Robin Hood's Merry
Men rather than a gang of shallow thinkers looking for an issue to
exploit." 74) AIM's continental confrontation may coincide with the
federal government's own continental strategy for "social peace".
The anticipated "white" paper on Indian policy may promise greater
participatory democracy. However, the Northern people should be
given real native rights without delays about national sovereignty.
The Native peoples should be given freedom and responsibilities
within Canada, rather than in the direction of an unstable,

independent nation between Canada and Russia.

In the wake of the Soviet Union's success in Angola, the Russian Communist Party praised leftist revolutionaries abroad and promised Third World liberation movements, "the consistent advocates of peace and security", support for their revolutionary wars. At the same time it affirmed East-West detente, the independence of communist parties, all united in the struggle against oppression. Solzhenitsyn cannot understand how, in the wake of Angola, any free leader can still defend detente. Likewise, a Czechoslovak communist, Arnosh Kolman, a member of the Russian Communist Party for fifty years, who recently resigned and sought asylum in Sweden, wrote Chairman Brezhnev:"While preaching about 'international detente' and 'peaceful coexistence', the Soviet Union in fact...prepares for aggressive wars. It keeps vast armies outside its frontiers, builds more and more military bases in Europe, Asia, and Africa...is carrying out ceaseless attempts...to establish its military and political overlordship in various corners of the earth...." 75)

A Russian pilot, who fled to Japan, warned that the Soviet Union has contingency plans to crash planes on enemy targets in China and the West. Eldridge Cleaver, former Black Panther Information Minister and champion of the Tricontinental strategy, said that his most astonishing education abroad was to be invited to meetings where the entire strategy to isolate and destroy the United States was freely discussed. "I've talked with generals from the Soviet Union and marshals from China. I've been present when they toasted the destruction of the United States. They carry on constant planning of surprise attacks. They are out to eliminate, if possible, but in any case, to surround and surpass and neutralize the United States."76)

Rather than applying his rigid radicalism to a changing world, the new realities (empirical facts) and revelations should shake Trudeau's international idealism. How many scientists in Russia have to be stripped of their citizenship and scholarship; how many Russian and Cuban scientists and scholars have to be caught in subversive activities in Canada before Trudeau will begin to realize that his scientific humanism is different from Soviet humanism and that there, consequently, is no foundation for genuine friendship? Perhaps Trudeau and his personal advisor, Ivan Head, would do well to (re-)read a 1948 speech on Canadian foreign policy by the late

Lester B. Pearson in which he warned of being fooled by seemingly improved Soviet intentions and the failure to distinguish between Soviet strategy and tactics. 77)

If Trudeau does not wish to take seriously the warnings of those given above, let him listen to the "wise" men in Red China, who watch the world scene with growing uneasiness and encourage joint military strength with America as a counter-balance to Soviet imperialism. Castro once sought an enlightened third option: independence from(imperialist) America, but ended up as a Russian colony, supported by the "mother" country to the tune of $500 million per year. How many Russian warships and intelligence-equipped trawlers - versus one American floundering oil tanker 78) - have to be in Canadian waters before there is a policy which will be able to defend Canada and enforce its sovereignty on newly acclaimed territorial waters?

In 1969 Trudeau told the House of Commons: "I am not interested in protecting a few Canadian cities if this means we will be consenting to a kind of policy which we think is dangerous to the world." 79) A primary responsibility of any national leader is to have a defence policy which can protect cities and coasts.

Trudeau refers to Canadian-American relations as "sleeping with an elephant." (CC,p.174) What will it be like sleeping with a hungry bear? If Russia were to succeed as well in its friendship with Canada as it has with Cuba, it will have succeeded in its ultimate objective: encirclement of the United States, backed up by its ever-growing sea power.

Trudeau has said that it is the responsibility of leaders to have the deepest understanding of the world. (CC,p.146) It appears that his vision has blocked out part of reality in international affairs. Vladimir Bukovsky told Peter Kent on CBC Newsmagazine "From Russia with Hate"(!!!) (March 7,1977) that he should like to meet the Prime Minister to complain about his toast in Norilsk, USSR in May 1971. Soviet intellectuals were horrified to read in *Pravda* that Trudeau considered Norilsk a model of northern development. Norilsk, according to Trudeau, "is surely one of the modern marvels of the world - and one which sets a standard in Arctic living for all other countries.... The level of accomplishment...is nothing short of spectacular." (CC,pp.146-147) According to Bukovsky, it was an awful mistake on Trudeau's part because he knows nothing about the real history of the place - how many prisoners perished to build this city. Even if he knew, Trudeau may shrug it off as an unfortunate side effect in the revolutionary history toward freedom and development. (AP, pp.74-75)

What is also significant, is that his foreign policy principles are morally radically different from previous Liberal and Conservative governments. From a liberal-conservative scale of values, his statesmanship has not reflected wisdom and understanding of national unity. It is one thing to give up sovereignty, but another to downgrade one's national identity. But, then, Trudeau does not attach lasting meaning to nations. Like the great historian Thucydides, Trudeau's greatness as an international leader may be that he is able to visualize a world in which Canada will be no more.(FFC, p.177)

Notes

1. **The Best of Trudeau,** p. 51.
2. Quoted in Stuebing, Marshall, and Oakes, **op. cit.,** p. 16
3. **Foreign Policy for Canadians,** 1970, pp. 21, 41-42.
4. Quoted in "Trudeau's Balancing Act," **Business Week,** November 1974, p.61. Trudeau has said that his policy towards the United States was developed years before the energy crisis and concern with conservation of raw materials and food supplies.
5. See Peter C. Dobell, **Canada's Search for New Roles,** 1972.
6. "An Appeal for Realism in Politics," **The Canadian Forum,** May 1964, p. 33.
7. **Ibid.,** p. 33; and **Foreign Policy for Canadians,** p. 28.
8. **Foreign Policy for Canadians,** p. 9.
9. Quoted in Dale C. Thomson and Roger F. Swanson, **Canadian Foreign Policy: Options and Perspectives,** p. 31.
10. "An Appeal for Realism in Politics," **op. cit.,** p. 33.
11. **Foreign Policy for Canadians,** p. 39.
12. Ivan Head, "Foreign Policy of the New Canada," **Foreign Affairs,** January 1972, Vol. 50, No. 2, p. 240.
13. J.L. Granatstein, "External Affairs and Defense," in John Saywell and Donald Forster, eds., **Canadian Annual Review** for 1970, p. 314.

14. Louis St. Laurent, "The Foundations of Canadian Policy in World Affairs," in Robert A. Mackay, ed., **Canadian Foreign Policy 1945-1954,** pp. 388-393.
15. J.F. Kennedy, **The Strategy of Peace,** edited by Allan Nevins, New York: Popular Library, 1961, p. 30.
16. David Halberstam, **The Best and the Brightest,** p. 814. New York: Random House, 1972. See also Richard J. Walton, **Cold War and Counter-Revolution,** Baltimore: Penguin Books, 1973.
17. **Foreign Policy for Canadians,** pp. 7, 29.
18. See Norman Podhoretz, "Making the World Safe for Communism," **Commentary,** April 1976, pp. 310-314. See also Walter Laqueur, "'Eurocommunism' and Its Friends,'" Commentary, August 1976, pp. 25-30.
19. Trudeau and Hebert, **op. cit.,** p. 66.
20. **Foreign Policy for Canadians,** p. 21.
21. James Eayrs,**Greenpeace and Her Enemies.** Toronto: House of Anansi Press Ltd., 1973, p. 339.
22. Trudeau and Hebert, **op. cit.,** p. 54.
23. **Ibid.,** pp. 66, 70.
24. **Ibid.,** p. 71.
25. **Ibid.,** p. 152.
26. **Ibid.,** pp. 3, 146.
27. See John Chang, **Industrial Development in Pre-Communist China.** Chicago: Aldine Publishing Co., 1969.
28. Trudeau and Hebert, **op. cit.,** p. 151.
29. **Ibid.,** She may no longer have the same attitude toward Trudeau, but correctly comments: "...if he goes down — he'll go down as his own man, clinging only to his principles, including those involving the press." "Endpiece," **Saturday Night,** December 1976, p. 92. What an admirable way to go down!
30. **The Toronto Star,** July 29, 1976, p. C1.
31. P.T. Bauer, "Western Guilt & Third World Poverty," **Commentary,** Vol. 61, No. 1 (January 1976) pp. 33-34.
32. **Ibid.,** p. 38.
33. **Ibid.**
34. **Ibid.**
35. W.W. Rostow, **Politics and the Stages of Growth,** pp. 11-12. Cambridge: Cambridge University Press, 1971.
36. **Foreign Policy for Canadians,** pp. 14, 25, 34.
37. See Bruce Thordarson, "Posture and Policy: Leadership in Canada's External Affairs," International Journal, Vol. XXXI, No. 4(Autumn 1976) p. 674. Even though Prime Minister Trudeau praised Pearson for his contribution to world affairs (CC, p. 157), Bruce Hutchison related that Pearson "was outraged" when Trudeau implied in a 1969 major speech that before Trudeau's government had reviewed and changed Canadian foreign policy, it had been mainly controlled by concepts of military men "— a brutal, unjustified attack on Mike's record, the very opposite of the truth, whether Trudeau knew it or not." Bruce Hutchinson, **The Far**

Side of the Street (Toronto: Macmillan) 1976, p. 352. Justified or not, Trudeau implicitly expressed the same radical critique of Liberal foreign and defense policy as he had explicitly stated in the April 1963 **Cite Libre** article "The Abdication of the Spirit" of "Pope Pearson".

38. Thordarson, **op. cit.**, p. 68.
39. Trudeau and Hebert, **op. cit.**, p. 151.
40. Thordarson, **op. cit.**, p. 162. A senior advisor to the Prime Minister claimed that it was not a compromise, but the "right decision." Nevertheless, it seems that Mr. Trudeau originally desired even greater cuts in Canada's NATO contribution and would have achieved them had he not encountered such stiff opposition in the Cabinet." (**Ibid.**, p. 158) The decision was a "right compromise." However, Liberal Senator John Black Aird resigned his chairmanship of the Canadian NATO Parliamentary Association, the association which advises Parliament on NATO policy. He knew the difference between the liberal and socialist meaning of "compromise" and since he could not in good, liberal conscience make such a compromise, he had the courage to resign.
41. **Ibid.**, p. 145.
42. There was "a conviction within NATO that any reduction in the size of a member's military contribution should not be made uni-laterally." The Harmel Report had been followed by the Reykjavik declaration of 1968, in which the member nations committed themselves to the goal of mutual and balanced force reductions (MBFR) with the Soviet Union. An important part of this communique was the implication that uni-lateral actions on the part of any member country would prejudice this search for arms limitations and detente in Europe. (**Ibid.**, p. 14)
43. **Maclean's,** September 6, 1976, pp. 19-20. See also "Who Rules the Waves?", **Maclean's,** February 7, 1977, pp. 26-30.
44. Quoted in **The Globe and Mail,** January 17, 1977, p. 8.
45. See John Gellner, "Gedenia Affair Reveals Absence of any Effective Canadian Control over Arctic Waters," **The Globe and Mail,** September 17, 1975; and his article in **The Globe and Mail,** October 15, 1974.
46. Alexander Solhzenitsyn, "Warning to the Western World," **Canadian Review,** September and October, 1976. Also available from SECA, Box 5966, Columbia, S.C.
47. Alexander Solhzenitsyn, "Warning to the Western World," **Ibid.**
48. The Soviet government pressured the CBC to censor Radio Canada International. Now people in Eastern Europe will no longer be able to hear how well immigrants from the Soviet Union are doing in Canada. They will no longer hear about the wages of Canadian workers and about the celebration of Christmas. **The Toronto Star** editorialized: "The behavior of the External Affairs department and the CBC which have thus bowed to Soviet complaints is scandalous.... What is at stake in this instance is Canada's freedom to report or to comment as it will on what we — not the Soviets — regard as newsworthy developments. It's outrageous to let this freedom be abridged by the Soviet ambassador.... It deserves nothing less than a thorough inquiry. "Shameful Retreat before the Soviets," **The Toronto Star,** August 13, 1976, p. B4.

49. Robert Nielsen, Opinion, **The Toronto Star,** September 15, 1976, p. C4. The documentary was about America as an imperialist power. See also Robert Nielsen, "The Big Lie About America," **The Toronto Star,** April 28, 1976. The interview with Solhzenitsyn was broadcast over TV Ontario, opposite a Canadian Cup hockey game.

50. J.F. Kennedy, **To Turn the Tide,** edited by John W. Gardner. New York: Popular Library, 1962, pp. 171, 68.

51. See Kenneth McNaught, "Foreign Policy," in Michael Oliver, ed., **Social Purpose for Canada,**   pp. 455-462; and **Foreign Policy for Canadians,** p. 5. Trudeau's new approach is much like that of the democratic   socialist H. Stuart Hughes. Hughes also offered a new foreign policy, a policy of uni-lateral disarmament and withdrawal from nearly all military alliances as an alternative approach to peace. Hughes also saw no need to fear communism or the Soviet Union, and saw a future world in which superpowers would hold varying degrees of control over "satellites". His perspective assumed total change of NATO as originally established. See H. Stuart Hughes, **An Approach to Peace.** New York: Atheneum, 1962. There are also parallels between Trudeau and James M. Minifie's **Peacemaker or Powermonkey** (Toronto: McClelland and Stewart, 1965), but Minifie is a principled neutralist, while Trudeau is no pacifist. (CC, p. 69)

52. An excellent study of the decision-making process in foreign policy has been written by Bruce Thordarson. It is highly recommended for those who desire more information in this area.

53. Thordarson, **op. cit.,** p. 135.

54. **Ibid.,** p. 136.

55. Ivan Head. "Foreign Policy of the New Canada," **op. cit.,** p. 250.

56. Denis Smith, "North American Ways," **The Canadian Forum,** October 1976, p. 4.

57. See Mel Watkins, "The North American Triangle," **The Canadian Forum,** February 1977, pp. 14-17.

58. Trudeau and Hebert, **op. cit.,** p. 152.

59. **Foreign Policy for Canadians,** pp. 7, 29. In Singapore on May 23, 1969, he referred to America's role in Asia as a "form of imperialism." J.L. Granastein, "The White Paper on Foreign Policy," in Saywell and Forster, **op. cit.,** p. 328.

60. Quoted by Ivan Head, "Foreign Policy of the New Canada," **op. cit.,** p. 246. In pursuit of his "Third Option", Trudeau did not make it an issue of trust when Japan and Common Market countries were primarily interested in our natural resources and expected us to buy manufactured goods.

61. Senator George C. Van Roggen, "The Government Dialogue — United States-Canada," November 9, 1976. Senator Van Roggen chaired the Standing Senate Committee hearings for an alternative institutional framework to Canada-United States relations.

62. K.R. Minoque, **Nationalism,** p. 138."They are both doctrines of struggle but they diverge fundamentally on the nature of the struggle." For a Marxist it is a class struggle, and for a nationalist it is an ethnic struggle.

63. Quoted by Andre Major, "Arms in Hand," in Scott and Oliver, eds., Quebec States Her Case, **p. 81.**
64. Abraham Rotstein, "Canada: The New Nationalism," **Foreign Affairs,** Vol. 55, No. 1 (October 1976) pp. 110-111.
65. **Ibid.,** p. 114.
66. W.A.Wilson, "Seeking Short-term Popularity," **The Montreal Star,** March 10, 1976.
67. **The Way Ahead,** p. 15.
68. **Foreign Policy for Canadians,** p. 28.
69. See Alan C. Cairns, "Political Science in Canada and the Americanization Issue," **The Canadian Journal of Political Science,** June 1975, Vol. 8, No. 2, pp. 202-212. See also Donald C. Rowat "The Decline of Free Research in the Social Sciences," **The Canadian Journal of Political Science,** December 1976, Vol. 9, No. 4, pp. 537-547.
70. Quoted by Cairns, "Political Science in Canada and the Americanization Issue," **op. cit.,** pp. 208-209.
71. **The Telegraph Journal,** January 30, 1976, p. 1.
72. See Robert Nielsen, "Trading Canadian dollars for Fidel's Kissing — and Spies," **The Toronto Star,** January 19, 1977, p. 4.
73. Quoted in **The Montreal Star,** February 26, 1976, p. 16.
74. Doug Cuthand, Letter to the Editor, **Maclean's,** November 15, 1976, p. 16. See also Ms. M. McDonald's article, **Maclean's,** October 18, 1976.
75. See Arnosh Kolman, "Open Letter," **The Montreal Star,** October 16, 1976, p. 6.
76. Laile E. Bartlett, "The Education of Eldridge Cleaver," **The Reader's Digest,** October 1976, p. 106.
77. See Lester B. Pearson, **Words & Occasions,** pp. 70-77. They should also read Andrei D. Sakharov's **My Country and the World** (1975), New York: Vintage Books; especially his warning to the Liberal intelligentsia of the West in Chapter five.
78. **Foreign Policy for Canadians,** p. 13.
79. **The Best of Trudeau,** p. 136.

"...there are no absolute truths in politics."
Trudeau, 1967

"You cannot tell lies to the people. They will
not believe you. People are more sophisticated now."
Trudeau, 1968

"Why did we lie to you? Unless we can explain
that the people...have the right to be mad...
the right to say this government has lost its
credibility."
Trudeau, 1976

Chapter 7
A Just Society

A new Spirituality of Politics

It is amazing how much Prime Minister Trudeau has accomplished in several decades. In the Preface of a book by Trudeau, Gerard Pelletier wrote: "I have no hesitation in saying that I consider Pierre Trudeau's work to be the most serious effort to formulate a political theory for Quebec and Canada that has been attempted in the past twenty-five years. Whether or not his conclusions, or even the general direction of his thought, are accepted, no one can deny the intellectual integrity that characterizes these essays, the exceptional erudition on what they are based, or the trenchant wit of his remarkable style." (FFC, p.xvi) There is certainly no quarrel with his intellectual integrity or competence. The problems arise with his "conclusions" and "general direction".

First of all, the Prime Minister has broken down the traditional foundations of authority and substituted new ones. The consequences of this radical shift in authority have far-reaching effects. Secondly, he has been less than fully honest (lacked political integrity) with the Canadian people and Parliament. Herein lies the loss of his credibility as a liberal leader. Responsibility for the future of Canada rests with each and every Canadian, but especially with politicians and the press.

In Quebec, Trudeau was actively engaged in removing the old bourgeoisie superstructure (Church, economic, political) which was, in his opinion, out of touch with reality. "Our official thinkers... ignored all the social science of their own day." (AS,pp.12-13) They "could not free themselves from a social environment that was traditionalist, anti-modern, and imbued with authoritarianism and fuzzy thinking." (AS,p.12) The industrial workers of Quebec "were suffocating in a society burdened with inadequate ideologies and oppressive institutions...." (AS,p.66) He explicitly rejected the traditional-ethical basis of authority: God, church, and nature.

It is one thing to champion the distinction between church and state, but quite another to divorce Christianity from public life. For Trudeau, the Christian religion is a private relationship between God and man, while politics is a public relationship of citizens. It is one thing for Trudeau to say that "the state has no business in the bedrooms of the nation". It is quite another to imply that God has no place in public life. The Ontario legislature opens every day with a beautiful prayer, but one wonders how many legislators pay more than lip service to the exercise. Perhaps the PQ government in Quebec is less hypocritical in its abolishment of prayers.

Trudeau's attitude has been consistent on the question of abortion, capital punishment, as well as on divorce legislation. With respect to broadening the grounds for divorce, he said on December 5, 1967: " I want to separate sin from crime. You may ask forgiveness for your sins from God, but not from the Minister of Justice." 1) The divorce of justice and politics from absolute Truth will eventually have disastrous consequences for Canada.

The Prime Minister has succeeded in separating Christianity from politics, only to reintroduce his own new public religion: social radicalism. For radicals, politics functions as a new religion. Like Mao, Trudeau wants to achieve through politics what is, in reality, possible only through Christianity: the making of a new man and a new society. For Trudeau, the politicized workers are the real upholders of "spiritual values". (AS,p.347) He has politicized cultural values, elevating them to a spiritual level. (FFC,p.34) Cultural values are spiritual when they reach the level of universal and human values rather than national and material. (FFC,p.29) It seems that the UNESCO's philosophy of scientific humanism is

Trudeau's true, public religion. In that light he appears to envision a Canadian charter of human rights.

However, it is necessary to maintain realism in this new universalism. There exists no universal agreement on the idea of universality guiding UNESCO. It was "politics", the radical politics of Russia and Arab countries, which expelled Israel from the European group in 1974. It was only after a protest meeting of prominent scientists and intellectuals from twenty-five free countries, who sought to uphold the liberal idea of the "universality of UNESCO" and the possibility of a "second and real UNESCO, true to its original Charter", that UNESCO's general conference in Nairobi (November 1976) reinstated Israel. Yet radical politics will continue to divide world humanism, such as the recent communist-sponsored resolution to curtail liberal freedom of the press.

Trudeau, too, has radicalized (radically changed) educational, scientific, and cultural objectives in Canada. He has stated that "the basis of a socialist ideology is to work out a certain set of human values", which will result in "minimum standards of the good life." (FFC,p.150) Culture is such an important aspect of the new international, human values that the "state must use its legal powers to compel the economic community to favour certain values that would otherwise be destroyed by the pressure of economic forces." (FFC,p.29) The Trudeau government has used its legal and advertising power to program the public into a new lifestyle. His government has intervened in economic matters to reform our attitudes, values, and institutions — there is even a desire to reform the capitalists themselves.

A New Morality of Power

Apparently, Trudeau is not interested in the moral foundation of authority. Modern science, not Christianity, is a more suitable foundation of the nation. He is not interested in setting forth a theology of law and politics, but a political psychology of sociology of law. (AP, p.57) According to Trudeau, "any given political authority exists only because men consent to obey it. In this sense, what exists is not so much the authority as the obedience. One can therefore say that the power of governments rests on a psychological disposition on most people's part to believe that it is good to obey and bad to disobey." (AP,pp.31-32)   With the above understanding of obedience, it is little wonder that Trudeau is so disposed toward psychological conditioning of people in new behaviour patterns, disciplining them into new attitudes and values. However, he cannot escape the question of morality. Rather than a philosophical criteria, he provides us with a psychological criteria of "good" and "bad" behaviour. Secular social science is the foundation of the new society. But still the moral question of who has authority remains: namely, who has the constitutional authority to make policy and legislation? Should that not be a duly constituted parliament rather than an unelected scientific elite? Little wonder that the power of Parliament is undermined if modern men of secular science undermine the very constitutional foundation of authority.

The underlying assumption is that the scientific and technical elite know how the economy or society operates, that knowledge is the new power, and that their power is being used for the public interest;   while politicians, labour leaders, and businessmen cling to outmoded concepts of industry and democracy, serving only powerful self-interest groups detrimental to the common good. One could, therefore, have anticipated the announcement of Hugh Faulkner, Minister of Science and Technology, in the fall of 1976, which stated that the Science Council of Canada will play a greater role in the post-control period. The technical competence of the Anti-Inflation Board will probably be transformed and expanded into some kind of scientific planning and policy board for industrial democracy. Not surprisingly, in the winter of 1977, a joint Commons-Senate Committee said that Parliament had lost power over decision-making and that government is trampling on the people's human rights. Trudeau may have politicized the bureaucracy, but decisions are no more public. Power has shifted to the scientific elite who have no constitutional authority. As long as public opinion can be manipulated to obey it, the will of the man who holds power will be law. Such "realpolitik" is dangerous for the political freedom of people and for the authority of politics in a so-called "just society".

To understand Trudeau's commitment to science and technology is to realize that radical social science has the appeal of a new secular religion. Radical science presumes to have discovered the universal law to meaning and direction of history.

Marxist humanism is not just an economic theory, but an ideology, a new theology of world history. As Schumpeter saw so sharply: "Marxism is a religion. To the believer it presents, first, a system of ultimate ends that embody the meaning of life and are absolute standards by which to judge events and actions; and, secondly, a guide to those ends which implies a plan of salvation and the indication of the evil from which mankind, or a chosen section of mankind, is to be saved."2)   Schumpeter drew a broad analogy between the world of religion and the historical materialism of Marxism. So, too, one could say that Marx became "the prophet" for great humanist statesmen like Lenin and Mao. On the occasion of his centennial, Lenin was declared the greatest humanist of the century by UNESCO.

The political approach of the Prime Minister has mainly centered in history. In high school, "the only politics I was taught was history".(FFC,p.xix) In the university, at home and abroad, he was taught in the broader social sciences, the economics of history, and the economic history of war, such as economic causes of World War II. He dealt with Quebec in federalism almost exclusively in terms of economic history rather than national aspirations. He made a "conscious choice" to work on the winning, progressive side of history against the reactionary tide of politics and economics in Quebec. The future, according to Trudeau, does not rest with nationalism or economic liberalism, but on the side of international socialism. The "peoples of the earth became more oriented towards the left,"(AS,p.339) and we "must go forward with the caravan of humanity or perish in the desert of time past." (AS,p.345) "Like everything else, the Canadian nation had to move with the times." The "wise socialist" will move with the "dynamics of history" and use federalism as a means toward radicalism. (FFC, pp. 197-198, 141,125) He invited the "working classes" to join him in the formation of a "new Left" Party in the move toward "social radicalism". (AS,p. 343)   As Prime Minister, he had invited Canadians to join him in the building of a "new society" at home which will be part of a new international economic order — "the road to progress lies in the direction of international integration". (FFC,p.202) Canadians do not have a manifest destiny of Pan-Canadianism, but Trudeau has chosen to provide Canadians with, what is basically, a manifest Marxist sense of world history. Unlike the late Liberal Prime Minister MacKenzie King, who still envisioned Canada's role as protector of our Christian civilization, Trudeau is one of the contemporary leaders who appears to make the world safe for international socialism. As Robert Heilbroner wrote about Marxist economists, "their persuasion is that we should line

up on the side of history, as they see it. It is not a blueprint of the
future which the Marxists try to sell us, but a sense of historical
participation, of joining the winning team, of riding the 'wave of the
future. ' " 3)

The course of world history is towards the Left, but one can
seize the time to accelerate these processes or subvert the
diversionary tactics of reactionary forces. Like Lenin in Russia,
radical intellectuals in "backward" Quebec can start a revolutionary
movement to overthrow a reactionary regime, which is mired in an
obsolescent superstructure. We are at the dawning of an age of new
humanism. (AS,pp.345-347)

When Trudeau went to China, he saw promising beginnings in
the East. He described Mao Tse-tung as "one of the great men of the
century... (with) a look of wisdom tinged with melancholy. The eyes
in that tranquil face are heavy with having seen too much of the
misery of men."4) At the passing away of Chairman Mao, Prime
Minister Trudeau said that Mao was a "giant of the 20th century",
the founding father of a "new China". "The People's Republic of
China stands as a monument to the spirit and political philosophy of
Chairman Mao. Though our social and political systems differ,
Canadians recognize the pathbreaking spirit of community that,
under Chairman Mao's guidance, has contributed to the modernization of China."

Trudeau finds it regretful that our history stresses the negative
aspects of revolution. "...it is deplorable that history as it has been
taught among us treats the great revolutions (French, Russian, etc.)
only in terms of their ill effects and never acknowledges that it is
possible to see them as struggles for liberty against injustice."
(AP,p.74) The struggle against injustice is commended — it is the
orientation and means which create the problem. Trudeau has yet to
learn the lesson that great revolutions never fail to generate tyranny
and degrade human dignity. (AP,p.75)

Yes, China illustrates the triumph of an idea, Marxist
humanism, but what had Mao really cccomplished other than staying
in power by destroying most of his comrades-in-arms and co-rulers of
China. He may have eliminated begging, unemployment, and
inflation, but at the human cost of an estimated 30-50 million of his
own Chinese people. Rather than "modernization" of the Chinese as
a community, Mao achieved collectivization by regimentation. Not
simply modernization, but a complete secularization of the new man

and society. In 1949 there were 3.2 million confessing Catholic Chinese Christians; three Catholic universities; 200 Catholic high schools; and 1850 Catholic elementary schools. In 1977 one finds only a few official churches with few worshippers. As Trudeau and Hebert reported, the churches in the new China are "empty" and the constitutional guarantee of religious freedom "totally meaningless".5) If one looks at other countries which have joined the caravan of humanity, such as the U.S.S.R. and Cuba, it appears that freedom to practice the Christian religion will not or cannot be one of the absolute human rights. Trudeau has written that the church does not deserve support if it cannot adapt Christianity to the new humanism of our time. (AS, p.347)

In liberal language, the idea of Red China as a "community" is tragic because it is constituted as a disciplined authoritarian society. The people have been made to "will" the goals that those in authority chose for them.6) In 1957 Mao tried to give more freedom of expression to the people, hoping that they would not criticize the foundations of the new society, but soon had to resort to discipline and tight controls before the situation got out of hand. If given a choice, most Canadians and Chinese might prefer to live in Canada with 5% unemployment and 10% inflation rather than in the people's paradise of Mao. John R. Roche of Tufts University has called China "certainly the largest and probably the most efficient concentration camp in history."7)

Trudeau has faith in industrialization and modernization; and has apparently opted for elements of the Marxist, socialist model as a reaction against the liberal capitalist mode. However, neither model can solve man's problems if it is rooted in a secular view of man and society. Prime Minister Trudeau appears to think that as long as we control inflation and plan our economy — with the assistance of a disciplined people — we shall have domestic peace. He has turned away from liberal economics, and has sought a solution in the direction of (Marxist-oriented) democratic socialism. However, former Marxist Alexander Solzhenitsyn rejects this solution as dead dogma and believes it is responsible for a reactionary regime which results in backwardness in Russia. While Trudeau has taken issue only with the liberal capitalist stage of industrialization, Solzhenitsyn radically questions the secular roots of modernization, capitalism, and Marxism. He calls for a return to a Christian basis of civilization: absolute Truth as the foundation for a society. Likewise, Trudeau could have more respect for the past, and worship less his vision of the future.

In the light of the new structure of a scientific elite, and his belief in leadership democracy, Trudeau fosters intolerance. From the heights of his superior intelligence and intuition, he looks down on the "stupidity" of the ordinary people, the do-nothing and know-nothing politicians, and the mediocrity of the opposition. Claude Ryan, editor of the nationalist *Le Devoir* a decade ago considered Trudeau "arrogant, intransigent", with a "detestable tendency to judge from ahigh and afar problems which he does not understand", and a "destructive rigidity, hostility and dogmatic lack of serenity."8) In 1976 Trudeau called Quebec Premier Robert Bourassa a fool for promoting "politically stupid" legislation. Quebec Liberal Finance Minister Ramond Garneau called Trudeau's speech "injustifiably violent and arrogant." 9) Prominant people of "plain living and high thinking," wrote Gilbert K. Chesterton, are in need of "high living and plain thinking." What matters in life, in political life, is the "simplicity of the heart" rather than the complexity of the mind of a man in sandals.10) One cannot be held responsible for one's intelligence, but should be held responsible for open displays of arrogance and intolerance.

Canadians are a people of moderation and tolerance (CC,pp.191,192,205,212), but Prime Minister Trudeau has displayed intolerance. He has called separatist intellectuals traitors, counter-revolutionaries who commit treason against the course of history. His many insults against Liberals are well known. In practice, if not theory, he appears to be committed to what the Marxist Herbert Marcuse called "Repressive Tolerance"; tolerance for Trudeau's radical ideas, but intolerance for more conservative and national aspirations. Trudeau has elaborated his position somewhat by stating: "But tolerance is only of benefit if it remains a positive force. It is evil if it becomes an excuse for inaction or lack of care." (CC,pp.212-213) Who decides the subjective question of "positive" versus a "negative" force? If one sees history as only one caravan heading left, tolerance may likewise become very limited in scope. In this sense, Trudeau's tolerance takes on a rather authoritarian character.

He has even threatened to take away the licence of a radio station if it became a vehicle for separatist propaganda. So much for freedom of expression! He would like to make the "dissemination of hate literature a criminal offence.''(CC,p.41) This desire was renewed early in 1977. Who defines "hate"? That could include literature by people who love their country, but strongly object to the left-of-liberal direction in which Trudeau is taking the nation. "This streak of intolerance is the one important quality," according to NDP House Leader Ed Broadbent, and "could prove to be of crucial, even of tragic significance to Canada's future."11) Such a statement from a House Leader, from someone who deals with the Prime Minister on an almost daily basis, may be prophetic.

The intolerance is not so much personal, as a principled impatience with narrow-minded and short-sighted people. As the late Hannah Arendt pointed out in her study of authoritarian and totalitarian regimes, the leader(ship) uses the people and their national economy for a higher goal (international social order) rather than for the benefit of his own people and nation.

Recently, columnist Richard Gwyn remarked, what others have observed as well, that Trudeau has an intense interest in concepts, but people are regarded more as means to serve his ideas. 12) The irony is not, however, that Trudeau is oblivious to the privileges of wealth, or his inability to identify with the people. Rather, it appears to be his consciousness of the privilege to serve as a world leader, his drive to identify with the poor people of the world to the point of indifference to his own country's political economy. He cares passionately that ideas should serve people, but in practice Canadians end up serving international ideas. For example, money from Canadian taxpayers is used to support a communist regime in Cuba at incredibly low interest rates, while Canadians must pay four times as much for their loans. It is no wonder that a London, Ontario small businessman has refused to pay that portion of his taxes which goes to support Castro's Cuba. In a similar vein, Trudeau is insensitive to the national aspirations of Quebeckers because of his vision of inter-nationalism.

Trudeau is to be commended for his commitment to justice rather than personal power. Justice "is a cornerstone of the society I live in, the basis of all human relations in the family or the state... the total of the relationships in a society of free men. The Just Society is the kind of society freedom would establish."(CC,p.12) Industrial democracy and equal distribution of wealth are preconditions of social justice. (AS,pp.338-339) Justice is one of the primary tasks of a government and we, therefore, deeply appreciate Trudeau's elevation of justice to a cornerstone of society.

The difference arises when the traditional foundations of justice are removed. If the search for justice is divorced from divine Truth and legislative law is separated from the Law of God and Nature, justice can only be attained by a subjective will and power (the will to power). To sever justice from all its traditional roots is to open the gates to vice and terror. In the name of social justice, Plato's superior statesman abolished personal property and family life for the public good. Plato's "just" state (AP,p.84) was a power state. Trudeau may thirst for righteousness (AS,p.349), but divorced from its Biblical roots, the result may be only the politics of self-righteousness or even unrighteousness. The Just Society will not be a society of equals. Social democrats may be committed to the "politics of equality" in a liberal society, but in a democratic socialist society, to use George Orwell's words: "some animals are more equal than others."

As mentioned earlier, the separation of God from the public life of a nation can have serious consequences. A British Prime Minister once said: "Justice is truth in action." But for Trudeau, "there are no absolute truths in politics." (FFC,p.xxii) The first law of politics is not great principles of truth, but facts. (FFC,p.8) If there are no absolute truths, then everything becomes possible and justice is merely a "roundabout way of applying the law of the stronger" in the form of an all-powerful Prime Minister. Truth may be turned into a lie and lying into truth.

The Prime Minister's effort to explain his deception of the electorate in 1974 is a moral outrage. "Why did we lie to you? Unless we can explain that the people outside the St. John Hotel have the right to be mad. Unless we can explain the flip-flop they have the right to say this government has lost its credibility."13) According to him, the problem in 1974 was an international one (oil price increases) and in 1975 it was domestic wage and price increases. But both domestic and international causes of inflation existed in 1974 and in 1975. The reversal on controls is said to be a necessary "flip-flop". But has Trudeau forgotten what he thought of Pearson's flip-flop in 1963?

Trudeau appears to have a somewhat functional use of deception in politics to serve a higher morality of the new society. But it is a "sin" against the spirit of liberal democracy to deliberately lead the people astray in a general election. Such maneuvers are even more objectionable from someone who believes in a leadership democracy which places high priority on accountability and on general elections. In 1961 Trudeau tried to persuade socialists and the NDP to stand for different things in various parts of Canada, in particular in Quebec. In the 1968 election he severely criticized the NDP for standing for different things in Quebec and the other provinces, and told the voters not to trust a leader and party which speaks out on two sides of the issue of federalism and the French-Canadians. Campaigning against Tommy Douglas, Trudeau said: "you can't tell lies to the people. They will not believe you. People are more sophisticated now."14) He appears to measure by double standards when he reminds the PQ government that it has no mandate to make a new nation, while he seems to have forgotten that the Canadian people gave him no mandate to build a new society. In trying to present a sophisticated explanation as to why there should be a controls period in 1975 rather than earlier when the electorate wanted one, Opposition Leader Robert Stanfield perceived that the Prime Minister had "spun a web, he's tangled in the web and oh, what a web it is!" He added: "No government can behave like this and maintain its credibility.... "15)

By 1977, people suddenly dislike Trudeau deeply because the public still places a high priority on (traditional) truth in politics. They do not necessarily want brilliant men or bright ideas, but boldness in the plain and simple truth. They want men and women who will tell them openly where the ship of state is going — not just vague references to a "new society" — since no one wants to sail on a Titanic. Although much of liberal politics may be secular, truth is still a high virtue in a liberal democracy. Lying in politics, wrote political scientist Kalman Silvert, "is the most nefarious political offense. One lies by imbuing the event with meaning one knows to be false. Untruths... destroy the possibility of creating common perceptions of political events and therefore can fracture a political community at all levels of participation."16) Nothing destroys a community spirit more quickly than deception.

People, Press and Parliament

It is by the consent of Canadians that the Prime Minister governs. In his own words, "when authority in any form bullies a man unfairly (think of examples such as "bludgeon" labour unionists, "threaten" radio station), all other men are guilty; for it is their tacit assent that allows authority to commit the abuse. If they withdrew their consent, authority would collapse."(AP,p.34) The reason

Trudeau's power has not completely collapsed by means of revolt or revolution, is that the Canadian people with their tolerance have considerable respect for the moral foundations of authority and the elected representative form of government. The vast majority will voice their displeasure and wait until the next election. Solzhenitsyn's call upon the Russian people is relevant to all people: "DO NOT TAKE PART IN THE LIE. DO NOT SUPPORT THE LIE."17)

A heavy responsibility for thorough and comprehensive coverage of all government activity and priorities rests with the mass media. To a large extent, men of the media were responsible for the build-up of the "new politician", failing to report critically Trudeau's vision for Canada in the framework of his writings. Mind you, Ian Urguhart (*Maclean's* Ottawa correspondent) describes Marxist economist Joseph Schumpeter as a "pro-free enterprise" economist.18) And, supposedly to clarify Schumpeter's background, Peter Brimelow (*Maclean's* business editor) wrote: "Schumpeter was one of the outstanding European-born economists who immeasurably strengthened the free market faction in U.S. academic circles earlier this century."19) Nowhere in his writings did Schumpeter seek to strengthen the free market. He concentrated on the inevitable collapse of capitalism, as Brimelow concurred. Schumpeter did stimulate socialist thinking among students like Trudeau. Even though Trudeau acknowledged Schumpeter's input on his thinking, Brimelow sought to explain away Trudeau's mention of Schumpeter as irrelevant to the issue. "Perhaps, after all, the key to Trudeau is not intellect but ego. Names and ideas are symbols, to be deployed for the response they evoke rather than because of any intrinsic interest or understanding. They bear no necessary relationship to each other, or to policy."20) Not only is the above explanation an insult to the intellect of the Prime Minister, but it contradicts what Trudeau said one year earlier in the same magazine. At that time Trudeau said that he entered politics mainly for the opportunity to work out his ideas into practice.

It appears that *Maclean's* editor Peter Newman might have some problems of objectivity in his coverage of Prime Minister Trudeau. There is the choice of words, timing, and phrases such as "when we knew each other" and "you once explained to me". Newman obtained a privileged interview (September 1975) on leadership democracy and the economy which was published concurrently with the anti-inflation speech of the Prime Minister

(October 1975). When Trudeau's credibility as Liberal leader faced an even greater test with the September 1976 Cabinet reshuffle, *Maclean's* wrote warmly about the renewal of Trudeau's leadership. Concerning the alienation between politicians and the public in the sixties, Newman wrote: "We had spent a hundred years trying to become a nation; now we were a nation and it was hell."21) Now that Trudeau presided over his own loss of credibility, and alienation between politicians and the people, Newman continued to have the same expectations of Trudeau's leadership. "Pierre Elliott Trudeau finds himself once again at the centre of Canadians' hopes and concerns... a kind of Buddhist monk in mufti, he faces the current emergency (including resignation of his finance minister) with a curious sense of inner repose. A cool man in a hot world... unfazed by the complaints of drift and inaction that swirl about his government."22) At a time when the country confronted critical choices, *Maclean's* sent its parliamentary expert and Trudeau-watcher, Walter Stewart out of the country.23) Top quality involves more than appearance. The above magazine has been mentioned specifically because it has given the impression that it is the duty of Canadians to read it. Let it, then, exercise its journalistic excellence, independent from any government or party beyond the shadow of a doubt.

It is desirable and important to have an independent national newsmagazine, but the recent question of *Time Canada* — a conservative-liberal international magazine with a Canadian edition — was more than a question of finances. The present operations of *Time* are more profitable than before. In addition, foreign ownership of *Time Canada* could hardly have been the issue, because Trudeau makes no moral distinction between Canadian and American capitalists. (FFC,pp.12,202) Most Liberal politicians saw it strictly in economic or emotional (national) terms rather than a principle of freedom of the press. Fortunately, several Liberals such as Simma Holt (Lib.-Vancouver-Kingsway), a former journalist and no lackey of Cabinet or Caucus, continued to champion the liberal principle of freedom of the press. She maintained that it was unjust and a dangerous precedent for a government to prescribe a 70-80% Canadian content.

Unfortunately, most politicians viewed it as a single issue, an isolated rather than world-wide phenomenon. In Nairobi (November 1976) the UNESCO Conference considered a draft resolution, sponsored by the Soviet Union, on basic principles governing the use of mass communications to strengthen world peace and international understanding. It would require governments to be "responsible for the activities in the international sphere of all mass media under their jurisdiction." The foreign press (U.S. and European) is being blamed for biased, negative reporting from Third World countries.

A related incident took place early in January of 1977. The Minister of Manpower and Immigration, Bud Cullen commented that a NBC-TV Weekend program on the Toronto racial situation was a "preconceived" American notion imposed on Canada. His notion was preconceived (prejudice) because he had not even seen the transcript. In addition, he commented at a time when the city faced racial tension which was extensively covered in the Toronto papers.

It was Cullen, as Minister of Revenue, who laid down the government guidelines on "Canadian content". This issue concerns freedom of the press, and not everyone is agreed on the meaning of "freedom". One-time China correspondent Theodore H. White asked Chairman Mao if he believed in freedom of the press. Naturally, he did. After the establishment of the People's Republic, White discovered what Mao really meant: namely, freedom for the proletarian press and none other, because it only reflects reality. After all, one cannot expect Mao to grant freedom of expression to instruments of oppression and error. For instance, in 1945 Mao considered *Reader's Digest* a threat to world peace. In 1975 *Reader's Digest* survived the first round by having sufficient Canadian ownership, but the principle and meaning of "Canadian content" will surface again, as long as the magazines are considered missionaries of the American Way.

Trudeau's own attitude towards the press should be well-known. He has written: "There is thus the danger that mass media — to the extent that they claim to reflect public opinion — constituted a vehicle of error, if not indeed an instrument of oppression. For my part, I have never been able to read newspapers without a sense of uneasiness, especially newspapers of opinion. They follow their customers and are therefore always lagging behind reality." (FFC,p.xxii) The Prime Minister's views on tolerance of institutions, such as the church, when they are not a "positive force", is no secret.(AS,p.347) Concentration on the bad news about the anti-inflation program is almost considered an abuse of freedom of the press. To counter these newspapers of negativism, he considered it "perfectly defensible" to use taxpayers' money to manipulate public opinion in favour of the program he has previously opposed. Rather than a liberal government reflecting public opinion, Trudeau educates the public to understand his reflections of reality. In addition, he apparently expects the mass media to reflect his lead, preparing the public for new attitudes, new behavioural standards and new economic structures of industrial democracy.

The government's determination to change people's values is also evident in the advertising blitz in the "Operation Lifestyle Program" dutifully described as "Dialogue on Drinking". Drinking is a problem, but change of human behaviour by government may be a greater problem of principle and morality. The Minister of National Health and Welfare, Marc Lalonde, is considering departmental proposals to look over magazine content before publication to delete ads or articles that may encourage pro-drinking lifestyles. Jonathan Webb, editor of *Canadian Review*, commented that Lalonde's proposals "threaten a level of governmental interference in the press, and in the lives of individual Canadians, that is clearly intolerable."24)

For a country like Canada, embarked on a radical redevelopment of its people, press performance as a "vehicle for error" versus truly reflecting reality becomes a most relevant question. The issue is urgent in a country where press freedom is only a convention. The liberal principle of press freedom is being challenged by the radical principle of a responsible, progressive press. The sharp attack on the media by Cabinet members on February 17,1977 was illiberal and a dangerous precedent. The order to the CRTC to investigate the CBC for not being a positive force has overtones of government intimidation of the media.

The free press should have been more critical in its coverage of the Trudeau government. Newspapers and magazines which heralded in the new leader — built up Trudeaumania — have put the people to sleep. To the extent that the media has been a vehicle of error about Trudeau, he has largely been the beneficiary.   Trudeau himself suspected that the press had much to do with his decision to seek the liberal leadership. According to Walter Stewart: "One reason the Trudeau government has been so well received lies in the fact that we have not been well informed by the press; there is no sign that the performance will get better in the near future."25) With important exceptions, the press now informs more, but not necessarily better. It has become more critical, but often in a personal way or on peripheral matters such as minor details of a press conference. The press has a rare opportunity to cover a leader who has a radically new vision for Canada, a vision which he has stated several decades ago and is currently transforming into practice. Not only must there be a critical analysis of each "building block", but also of the envisioned final structure.

Besides the liberal press, Parliament must also hold the government accountable. This includes the loyal opposition as well as the government backbenchers who are loyal to the liberal tradition. In the caucus, Liberal members have a particular challenge to maintain Cabinet accountability.

Since the 1974 elections, there have been three major Cabinet shuffles and each time the quality suffered. Fewer men of stature are left to be a counter-weight for Trudeau at the level where it counts. Blind ambition, boundless ego, and short-sightedness on the part of too many has enabled Trudeau to triumph and survive. Consider the case of Liberal MP Bud Cullen. In 1975 Trudeau gave him a Cabinet position to appease the restless backbencher. Barely a year in his ministerial position, the Prime Minister shifts him and others around in the 1976 major reshuffle. The new minister of Manpower and Immigration said in an interview: "I rather thought I would be left in national revenue because I've been there just under a year and felt that as a new minister I had to get my feet a little wetter. I guess the hard work paid off. I think Mr. Trudeau felt that given the high profile of manpower and immigration it was a big job that needed doing and I suppose he looked around for someone who he thought could do the job. I guess that's when his eyes lit upon me."26) Allan MacEachen's fate was worse. He did not want to leave External Affairs. "I felt I was just getting it all together at External."27) Expecting to make External Affairs the summit of his political career, and gaining in stature as a humanitarian, he was shocked when the Prime Minister asked him to give up his post and return to being House Leader. The move was made to sound like a promotion, but, facing one of those famous third options, he reluctantly moved back to his former position. Said MacEachen: "Who the hell knows anything about politics anyway?"28) In the long term objectives, the move was prompted not so much to save the House that Trudeau built, but to save his leadership.

As scandals and resignations rocked the Cabinet, life-long

Liberals left the Party in droves. Prominent names come to mind of those who have resigned positions or left the Party: Judy LaMarsh, Tom Cossit, Perry Ryan, Paul Hellyer, Peter Cadeau, John Turner, Bud Drury, Mitchell Sharp, James Richardson, Gerard Pelletier, Jean Marchand, and Bryce Mackasey.29) Paul Theriault, national president of the Young Liberals of Canada, was no flunkey and yes man. He resigned in 1974, giving the following reason: "I became aware that certain small and elitist groups controlled party organizations and were able to direct and even subvert the will of the rank-and-file membership."30)

When one looks at the Cabinet there is a long list of those who retired, voluntarily or under pressure. There are no Liberals of stature left. How many were no longer needed by the Prime Minister, and how many resigned out of loyalty to liberalism? How far should Cabinet solidarity go before it becomes an "academic issue"? At least Jean Marchand, former Minister of Environment, knew the difference between solidarity with the workers and solidarity to a bourgeois tradition, the difference between compromise in practice and as a principle. On account of the 1976 summer settlement of bilingualism for the Quebec air controllers, he resigned because he felt that under the circumstances, it would not be possible for him to respect the principle of Cabinet solidarity.31) Trudeau respects men of principle like Marchand and after a brief interval, Trudeau rewarded his sincerity and solidarity with a Senate seat. On the issue of bilingualism in the airlines, Trudeau may have tactically retreated, but is determined to settle the issue in the right direction at the right time.

Bryce Mackasey's resignation from the Cabinet was not unexpected. After pleading for the exemption of the striking postal workers from the controls program (with the Prime Minister's tacit approval), and after the spontaneous applause he received at the 1975 Liberal Policy Convention (with the visible disapproval of the PM), Mackasey had become a liability — a rival power in the place of Turner. He had served his usefulness for Trudeau. Suddenly this giant in the Liberal Party, "the last of the red-hot Liberals", with a following of his own in the Party, disappeared in the September 1976 Cabinet reshuffle, supposedly because of the right-wing turn of Trudeau on banking legislation and the opportunity to make more money in private business.32) Rather than "defy something much more temporal: the Canadian big business establishment",

Mackasey, who wanted to be on the Cabinet's Priorities and Planning Committee, may have defied something more permanent, namely, the powers and radical program of the Prime Minister. Perhaps he began to realize that Trudeau's "new society" is something other than the "good old-fashioned free enterprise system made to work as it should. "33)

Trudeau is not about to resign as Prime Minister. At Harrison Hot Springs (1970) he said that a policy convention must not be considered a test of power within the Liberal Party, and the Liberal Party has not voted for a leadership convention. On several occasions in the past two years he has repeated his determination to stay, even if he were to lose five Quebec by-elections in the Spring of 1977. The year before he warned: "If I found in my own liberal ranks that a certain number of guys wanted to cut my throat... I'd make sure I cut their throats first. "34) In politics he apparently does believe in cut-throat competition. In addition, he has stated that he would only consider resignation if the next leader were committed to his policies and programs.

The Prime Minister has firm control over the government, but no longer over the Liberal Party. If he had firm control there would have been no need for the executives of the federal Liberal Party in Ontario and Quebec to reaffirm (in mid January 1977) "the leadership of Prime Minister Pierre Trudeau, vigorously and unanimously." There is widespread dissatisfaction with his liberal leadership in the Party.

Rather than leaving the Liberal Party or Cabinet like disgruntled individuals, those who are dissatisfied could act as party members. For when a Liberal spokesman like John Turner acts as an individual, he is criticized for self-serving "grandstanding". After all, a party is a "joint endeavor". Liberals could act like Trudeau, Pelletier and Marchand did when they joined the Party as a "team". To stop the erosion of the Party in numbers and liberal principles, a new team of "three wise men", such as Messrs Mackasey, Turner, and Gray (Lib.-Windsor) could make a joint declaration that they have lost confidence in the liberal leadership and call for a leadership convention. On the same day as the PQ victory, Quebec MP Harold Herbert (Lib.-Vaudreuil) sent a letter to members of the Liberal caucus stating that there was "an urgent need to discuss and act" on the leadership, because next year may be too late." The letter continued: "The actions of our own Prime Minister and the actions of our own federal party are being questioned by our members. It is my firm conviction that open frank discussion and decision-making leading to action is essential today if we are going to win the next election."35) Herbert mistakenly assumed that there would be an automatic vote on a leadership convention next year. Was not the November 1975 Policy Convention the real opportunity to have voted for such a convention? The Party might have fared better in 1976 by-elections and opinion polls if it had exercised democratic control over the leadership. All that the Liberal delegates to the March 1977 Party Workshop were permitted to do was to criticize the Trudeau government as elitist, secretive, and remote. As Liberals, they want responsibility, but Trudeau tells them the country needs "discipline". The Liberal Party appears to have an instinct on how to self-destruct.

Despite the loss of credibility, confidence, and by-elections, Trudeau continues in office. As long as he has the numerical majority, he may continue "applying the law of the stronger, in the form of the law of the more numerous."(AP,p.88) However, in these unique times, in which precedents and traditions are routinely broken, liberal members of Parliament, out of a sense of survival or solidarity with traditional liberalism, may cross the aisle to provide a counter-weight to Trudeau's sort of liberalism. Such a demonstration of loyalty to liberalism and democracy and priority of principle over power, would require a firm conviction and courage. It may be one of the few democratic options open if Trudeau feels the same way about a general election as he and Lalonde do about by-elections — Lalonde said (January 1977) that it would "not be responsible" to hold the by-elections at the present time. They may also consider it not responsible to hold a general election before a Quebec referendum. Even a Supreme Court may rule that the political crisis requires strong continuous leadership without the disruptions of a general election.

The danger has gone beyond the self-destruction of the Liberal Party — the country is on a course of self-destruction. The criteria for championing Trudeau as a leadership candidate in 1968 was that he could unify the country, unite the Liberal Party, master Parliament, and win the next election. If an election were held in 1977-78, he could still win it. However, he has stripped Parliament of important powers and prestige, divided the Liberal Party, and worst of all, divided the country as never before. This possibility was already envisioned by NDP leader Tommy C. Douglas on June 20,1968 — the man Trudeau accused of lying to the people. Douglas accused Trudeau of

" dividing this country as it has not been divided for a long time." 36) Trudeau wants to be a great distributor of wealth among regions, but has become the great divider. He wants to share economic power, but not political power — and all decisions are ultimately political ones. He has intense feelings in relation to English Canadians, but may yet turn Canada, economically, into another England. His politics of confrontation has confused conservatives, liberals, and socialist parties; created near chaos in the country and the economy and conquered Parliament for his purposes. Trudeau tells the Liberals at the March 1977 Workshop: "It is the degree of self-interest which seems to obliterate almost any feeling of community.... It is the unwillingness to compromise... which makes the survival of a united country difficult. That is why we are now in a crisis situation." Rather than Liberal self-interest, it is his confrontation politics which have polarized social groups and obliterated national unity. Differences between French and English Canadians, provincial and federal governments are polarized to the point of distrust and disunity. His policies of bilingualism have turned Liberal prejudices into adversary community relations. As former Cabinet member James Richardson told the delegates, "The great paradox of our time is that a federal government that claims to fight separatism is in itself contributing to the growth of separatism." There is an unwillingness to compromise, except in Trudeau's direction. We are in a crisis situation, because of the politics of crisis and a philosophy of confrontation rather than a liberal-conservative consensus. Under what other circumstances would one hear calls for a radical new deal and extra-parliamentary means to meet the crisis?

Although a welcome relief for many, replacing Trudeau with a Marc Lalonde, Jean Chretien, or a John Turner, or even the Liberal Party with the NDP or PC Party will not necessarily solve our problems. The problem is even greater than keeping Quebec in confederation. The problem is not one of personalities or policies, but principles — it is a question of fundamental values. The fate of Canada is currently in the control of Prime Ministers — Trudeau and Levesque — who attach no lasting meaning to Canada as a nation. Will all of Canada become a "sick society"? Social radicalism is not a solution, but essentially is part of the deterioration of fundamental values: of truth, honesty, integrity, consensus and community. The future of Canada is part of a larger crisis of values in the world — the sensate values of liberalism and Marxism. As the Russian sociologist

Pitirim A. Sorokin wrote some time ago: "the main issue of our times is not democracy versus totalitarianism, not liberty versus despotism; neither is it capitalism versus communism, not pacifism versus militarism, nor internationalism versus nationalism, nor any of the current popular issues daily proclaimed by statesmen and politicians, professors and ministers, journalists and soapbox orators.... It was not the Hitlers, Stalins, and Mussolinis who created the present crisis: the already existing crisis made them what they are — its instrumentalities and   puppets. They may be removed, but this removal will not eliminate the crisis nor even appreciably diminish it. It will merely create new super-Hitlers and Stalins, Churchills and Roosevelts, as long as the crisis lasts."37)

The future of world history lies in the direction of the civitas dei not the *Cite Libre* of the old or new Left. A city or nation built on an adoration of man cannot endure. Trudeau's dream of creating a new man and society through politics may culminate in a national nightmare, a new enslavement to disciplined democracy. Under his leadership democracy Canadians may sacrifice far more than anticipated. The final caravan of history is moving in the direction of the civitas dei . The real revolution in the world is Christianity, the coming and return of the Lord of History. Trudeau's march with the New Left is counter-revolutionary. He is a reactionary because he is on the wrong side of history. It is a personal tragedy that such a gifted man, who is so dedicated, can be so mistaken in his sense of history. A national regeneration of our Christian roots is required in Canada, lest we lament the degeneration of a nation.

Notes

1.   Quoted in Newman, **op. cit.**,p. 444.
2.   Schumpeter,**op. cit.,** p. 5.
3.   Robert Heilbroner, **The Worldly Philosophers,** pp. 290-291.

4. Trudeau and Hebert, **op. cit.,** p. 71.
5. **Ibid.,** pp. 42, 140.
6. Schram, **op. cit.,** p. 52.
7. John R. Roche, "But, What Exactly Did Mao do?" in **The Boston Herald American,** September 16, 1976, p. 18.
8. Quoted in Sullivan, **op. cit.,** p. 252.
9. Quoted in **The Telegraph Journal,** March 8, 1976, p. 1.
10. Gilbert K. Chesterton, "On Sandals and Simplicity," **Heretics,** London: John Lane Co. 1905, p. 137.
11. Ed Broadbent, **The Liberal Rip-Off,** p. 7.
12. See Richard Gwyn, "The Decline of the Trudeau Empire," **The Canadian Weekend Magazine,** November 27, 1976.
13. **The Toronto Star,** September 23, 1976, p. 11.
14. Quoted in Peacock, **op. cit.,** p. 357.
15. **The Telegraph Journal,** January 21, 1976, p. 1. On May 23, 1974 Stanfield opened his campaign in Winnipeg criticizing the credibility of the Prime Minister. "The record shows that he is neither credible as a witness nor bearable as an alternative... the worst thing that can happen to a government or leader of a government is to prize power more than truth." **Canadian News Facts,** Vol. 8, no. 74, June 1974, p. 1207. According to Stanfield it breaks down trust between the electorate and the elect leader. See **Maclean's** February 23, 1976, p.5.
16. Kalman Silvert, **Man's Power: A Biased Guide to Political Thought and Action,** New York: The Viking Press, 1970, p. 152.
17. Alexander Solzhenitsyn, et al., **From Under the Rubble,** p. 274, Toronto: Little Brown, 1975.
18. **Maclean's,** September 6, 1976, p. 19.
19. **Maclean's,** September 20, 1976, p. 48.
20. **Ibid.** Trudeau is much more consistent and thorough than Brimelow believes. Trudeau does not just throw names around, but carefully selects the names of modern social scientists. (AS, p. 13) See also **Two Innocents in Red China,** p. 113. There are many close parallels of thought between teacher (Schumpeter) and student (Trudeau) as we have shown in this study. Also, Brimelow brings about a false dilemma between Trudeau's "intellect" and "ego". While not claiming that both explain him, there really is no conflict, because Trudeau is a selfless intellectual. Here is another example of someone claiming to know better than Trudeau what the Prime Minister meant to say. It is rather disturbing that a business editor of a national magazine fails to understand the essential direction of Trudeau's thoughts and actions.
21. Newman, **op. cit.,** p. xi.
22. **Maclean's,** October, 1975, p. 4. According to Newman, Canada became a nation in the sixties, but now he places the country back in childhood, calling for extra-parliamentary channels to move towards a new nationalism and to bring about a cultural revolution in English Canada as well. See **Maclean's,** January 10, 1977, p. 10.
23. In 1972 when Stewart wrote his critical study of Trudeau's leadership, Newman immediately wrote to Trudeau, distantiating himself from his

fellow editor. Valuing truth more than power, Stewart had the integrity to offer his resignation. Marc de Villiers, "The National Dream of Peter C. Newman," **Weekend Magazine**, October 9, 2976, pp. 4-7.

24. **The Canadian Review,** December 1976, p. 6.

25. Stewart, **op. cit.,** p. 221.

26. **The Sarnia Observer,** September 15, 1976, p. 1. Mr. Cullen greeted the 1977 New Year with a press announcement that the Prime Minister planned to run again. "Thank you," commented **The Globe and Mail** (January 7, 1977, p. 6) "Your assurance that Prime Minister Trudeau will lead the Liberal Party in the next election was exactly what the country needed to steady it in these times of deceit and dissension. With the old massah galluping on, what have we to fear?"

27. **Maclean's,** October 4, 1976, p. 22. Donald Jamieson told Peter Desbarats, on Global TV **In Private Life** (March 6, 1977) that his appointment to External Affairs came as a surprise, because he fitted right in at Trade and Commerce and expected to stay there. However, he accepted the Prime Minister as the arbiter in all those matters. Jamieson said that you either take it or leave it; so he took it.

28. **Maclean's,** November 1, 1976, p. 40.

29. "There were so many crises, scandals, insinuations and resignations, so much bumbling, fumbling and folly, that many people who braved the decade through... became permanently glazed of eye and shaky of limb, like shell-shock victims." Christina Newman, "The Longest-Established Permanent Floating Chaos," **Saturday Night,** December 1969, p. 22. The decade she described was the sixties, but it could have been the seventies. She appears to be preoccupied with politician watching — what Trudeau and Levesque will do to each other — rather than with what it all means. See "The Exotic Mindscape of Pierre Trudeau," **Saturday Night,** January-February, 1977, pp. 17-23. She may no longer have the same attitude toward Trudeau, but correctly comments: "...if he goes down — he'll go down as his own man, clinging only to his principles, including those involving the press." "Endpiece," **Saturday Night,** December 1976, p. 91. What an admirable way to go down!

30. **The Winnipeg Free Press,** June 21, 1974, p. 8. "'Shortly after becoming involved I became aware of certain practices which struck me as somewhat unethical.... In my idealism I felt that I could change these and, to a degree, I did succeed in doing so, at least in the Liberal youth movement... Increased bureaucratization under Liberal governments is no accident. The party itself is under complete bureaucratic control. The elected officers of the party have become meaningless and superfluous. The national executive, responsible to the party at large, is completely powerless in any political sense. It simply acts as a rubber stamp for decisions made by a bureaucratic and technocratic elite. This is not the manner of running a party which is supposedly responsible to its members and to the public.'"

31. **Canadian News Facts,** Vol. 10, No. 12, July 4, 1976, p. 1593.

32. **Maclean's,** August 1976, p. 10.

33. Rather than speculate on whether MacKasey jumped and Turner was

pushed out, it is well to remember that Trudeau is in full control of Cabinet shuffles. Asked by a long-time associate if he found it difficult to fire people, "Trudeau said it wasn't as hard as he had anticipated. Then within hearing of a couple of other Ministers, he said with a mischievous smile, 'I think I may even try it again soon.' The Ministers, unsure whether this was entirely whimsy, made a quick retreat." Gerald Clark, "From Trudeaumania to Political Maturity," **The New York Times Magazine,** November 3, 1974, p. 72. This article, published in **The Reader's Digest** under the title: "Will the Real Pierre Please Stand Up?" is worth reading. (April 1975).

34. Quoted in **Maclean's,** June 28, 1976, p. 16.
35. Quoted in **The Montreal Star,** November 19, 1976, p. 1.
36. **Canadian News Facts,** Vol. 2, No. 12, July 4, 1968, p. 100.
37. Pitirim A. Sorokin, **The Crisis of Our Age,** pp. 22-23, New York: Dutton and Co. 1941.

Selected Bibliography

Black, Edwin R., **Divided Loyalties: Canadian Concepts of Federalism,** Montreal: McGill-Queen's University Press, 1975.

Burns, R.M. ed., **One Country or Two?** Montreal: McGill-Queen's University Press, 1971.

Broadbent, E., **The Liberal Rip-Off: Trudeauism vs. the Politics of Equality,** Don Mills: New Press, 1970

Chaput, Marcel, **Why I am a Separatist,** Toronto: Ryerson Press, 1962.

Clarkson, Stephen, ed., **An Independent Foreign Policy for Canada?** Toronto: McClelland and Stewart, 1968.

Christian, William, and Colin Campbell, **Political Parties and Ideologies in Canada,** Toronto: McGraw-Hill Ryerson, 1974.

Crepeau, P.A., and C.B. Macpherson, **The Future of Canadian Federalism,** Toronto: Macmillan Co., 1965.

Cook, Ramsay, **Canada and the French-Canadian Question,** Toronto: Macmillan, 1966.

Diefenbaker, John, **Those Things We Treasure,** Toronto: Macmillan, 1972.

Dobell, Peter C., **Canada's Search for New Roles: Foreign Policy in the Trudeau Era,** Toronto: Oxford University Press, 1972.

Eayrs, James George, **Greenpeace and her Enemies,** Toronto: House of Anansi Press, Limited, 1973.

Eayrs, James George, **Diplomacy and its Discontents,** Toronto: University of Toronto Press, 1971.

Foreign Policy For Canadians, Ottawa: Information Canada, 1970.

Fox, Paul W. ed., **Politics: Canada** Third Edition, Toronto: McGraw-Hill, 1970.

Gellner, John, **Bayonets in the Streets,** Don Mills: Collier Macmillan, 1974.

Gotlieb, Allan ed., **Human Rights, Federalism, and Minorities,** Toronto: Canadian Institute of International Affairs, 1970.

Grant, George P., **Lament for a Nation,** Toronto: McClelland and Stewart, 1970.

Harbron, John D., **This Is Trudeau,** Don Mills: Longmans, 1968.

Hockin, Thomas A. ed., **Apex of Power: The Prime Minister and Political Leadership in Canada.,** 2nd ed., Prentice-Hall, 1971, 1977.

Innis, Hugh R., **Bilingualism & Biculturalism,** An abridged version of the Royal Commission Report, Toronto: McClelland and Stewart, 1973.

Laurendeau,Andre, **Witness For Canada,** Translated by Philip Stratford, Toronto: Macmillan Co., 1973.

Mackay, Robert A., **Canadian Foreign Policy 1945-1954, Selected Speeches and Documents,** Toronto: McClelland and Stewart, 1970.

MacKirby, K.A., J.S. Moir, and Y.F. Zoltvany, eds.,**Changing Perspectives in Canadian History,** Don Mills: J. Dent and Sons, 1971.

Martin, Paul, **Paul Martin Speaks For Canada,** Toronto: McClelland and Stewart, 1967.

Meisel, John, **Working Papers on Canadian Politics,** Second enlarged edition, Montreal: McGill-Queen's University Press, 1975.

Moon, R., **PM/Dialogue,** Hull, Quebec: High Hill Publishing House, nd.

Newman, Peter, **The Distemper of our Times,** Toronto: McClelland and Stewart, 1968.

Newman, Peter, **Home Country, People, Places, and Power Politics,** Toronto: McClelland and Stewart, 1973.

Oliver, Michael ed., **Social Purpose For Canada,** Toronto: University of Toronto Press, 1961.

Peacock, Donald, **Journey to Power,** Toronto: Ryerson Press, 1968.

Pearson, Lester B., **Words and Occasions,** Toronto: University of Toronto Press, 1970.

Penniman, Howard R. ed., **Canada at the Polls,** Washington, D.C : American Enterprise Institute for Public Policy Research, 1975.

Possony, Stefan F., **Lenin Reader,** Chicago: Henry Regnery Co., 1960.

Rioux, Marcel and Yves Martin, eds. **French Canadian Society,** Toronto: McClelland and Stewart, 1969.

Rotstein, Abraham and Gary Lax, **Getting It Back: A Program for Canadian Independence,** Toronto: Clarke, Irwin, 1974.

Schram, Stuart, R., **The Political Thought of Mao Tse-tung,** New York: Frederick A. Praeger, 1963.

Scott, Frank and Michael Oliver,eds., **Quebec States Her Case,** Toronto: Macmillan Co., 1964.

Saywell, John ed., **Canadian Annual Review,** Toronto: University of Toronto Press, 1969-1976.

Sloan, Thomas, **Quebec, The Not-So-Quiet Revolution,** Toronto: Ryerson Press, 1965.

Stewart, Walter, **Shrug: Trudeau in Power,** Don Mills: New Press, 1972.

Stewart, Walter, **Divide and Con: Canadian Politics at Work,** Don Mills: New Press, 1973.

Stuebing, Douglas, John Marshall and Gary Oakes, **Trudeau, A Man For Tomorrow,** Toronto: Clarke Irwin, 1968.

Sullivan, Martin, **Mandate '68,** Toronto: Doubleday of Canada, 1968.

Tarnopolsky, Walter S., **The Canadian Bill of Rights,** Second revised edition, Toronto: McClelland and Stewart, 1975.

Taylor, Charles, **The Pattern Of Politics,** Toronto: McClelland and Stewart, 1975.

Thomson, Dale C., and Roger F. Swanson, **Canadian Foreign Policy,** Toronto: McGraw-Hill, Ryerson, 1971.

Thordarson, Bruce, **Trudeau and Foreign Policy,** Toronto: Oxford University Press, 1972.

Thorson, J.T. **Wanted a Single Canada,** Toronto: McClelland and Stewart, 1973.

Trudeau, P.E., **Federalism and the French Canadians,** Toronto: Macmillan,

1968. Translated by Joanne L'Heureux, Patricia Clayton, and The Montreal Star.

Trudeau, P.E., **Approaches to Politics,** translated by I.M. Owen, Toronto: Oxford University Press, 1970.

Trudeau, P.E., **Conversation with Canadians,** Toronto: University of Toronto Press, 1972.

Trudeau, P.E., **The Best of Trudeau,** Toronto:Paguarian Press Ltd., 1972.

Trudeau, P.E., ed., **The Asbestos Strike,** Translated by James Boake, Toronto: James Lorimer & Co., Publishers, 1974.

Trudeau, P.E. and Jacques Hebert, **Two Innocents in Red China,** translated by I.M. Owen, Toronto: Oxford University Press, 1968.

Trudeau, P.E., "Economic Rights," **McGill Law Journal,** Vol. 8, No. 2, 1961, pp. 121-125.

Westell, Anthony, **Paradox: Trudeau as Prime Minister,** Scarborough: Prentice-Hall, 1972.

Zink, Lubor, **Trudeaucracy,** Toronto: Toronto Sun Publication, 1972.

Zolf, Larry, **Dance of the Dialectic,** Toronto: James Lewis & Samuel, 1973.

Acknowledgements

Acknowledgement is made to the following publications and individuals for material quoted in this book.

Canadian`Institute of International Affairs, **Human Rights, Federalism, and Minorities** by Allan Gotlieb.

Clark Irwin, **Trudeau: A Man for Tomorrow** by Douglas Steubing, John Marshall and Gary Oakes.

Collier Macmillan, Canada Ltd., **Bayonets in the Streets** by John Gellner. Doubleday, from **Mandate '68** by Martin Sullivan. Copyright (c) 1968 by Martin Sullivan. Reprinted by Permission of Doubleday & Co., Inc.

Harper & Row, **Capitalism, Socialism, and Democracy** by Joseph A. Schumpeter.

House of Anansi Press, **Greenpeace and her Enemies,** 3rd ed., edited by Paul W. Fox; **Why I am a Separatist** by Marcel Chaput; **Journey to Power** by Donald Peacock.

James Lorimer & Co., **The Asbestos Strike,** edited by Pierre E. Trudeau, translated by James Boake.

Macmillan of Canada, **Federalism and the French Canadians** by Pierre E. Trudeau, translators Joanne L'Heureux, Patricia Clayton and **The Montreal Star; Witness for Quebec** by Andre Laurendeau, translated by Philip Stratford; **Quebec States her Case,** edited by Frank Scott and Michael Oliver. Reprinted by permission of the Macmillan Co. of Canada Ltd.

McClelland and Stewart, **Canadian Foreign Policy 1945-1954,** edited by Robert A. Mackay; **The Distemper of our Times** by Peter Newman; **French Canadian Society,** edited by Marcel Rioux and Yves Martin; **The Canadian Bill of Rights,** 2nd ed., by Walter S. Tarnopolsky; **The Pattern of Politics** by Charles Taylor; **Wanted a Single Canada** by J.T. Thorson.

New Press, from **The Liberal Rip-Off** by Ed Broadbent; and **Shrug: Trudeau in Power** by Walter Stewart. Used by permission of the authors and New Press, Don Mills, Ontario.

Oxford University Press, **Approaches to Politics** by Pierre E. Trudeau, translated by I.W. Owen; **Two Innocents in Red China** by Pierre E. Trudeau and Jacques Hebert, translated by I.M. Owen; **Trudeau and Foreign Policy** by Bruce Thordarson.

Pagurian Press, Ltd., **The Best of Trudeau**, copyright and reprinted by permission.

Praeger Publishers, **The Political Thought of Mao Tse-tung** by Stuart R. Schram.

Prentice-Hall of Canada, from **Apex of Power**, 2nd ed., edited by Thomas A. Hockin, c. 1971, 1977 by Prentice-Hall of Canada.

H. Regnery Co., **Lenin Reader**, edited by Stephen T. Possony.

University of Toronto Press, **Conversation with Canadians** by Pierre E. Trudeau; **Social Purpose for Canada**, edited by Michael Oliver; **The Canadian Annual Review**, edited by John Saywell.

Magazines, newspapers and media: **Canadian Forum; Canadian Press; Canadian Review; Cite Libre;** CBC; CTV; **Commentary; Financial Post; Foreign Affairs; The Globe and Mail; Maclean's; McGill Law Journal; The Montreal Star; The New Yorker; The New York Times Magazine; Reader's Digest of Canada; The Sarnia Observer; Saturday Night** and Christina McCall Newman; **The Toronto Star;** (St. John's) **Telegraph Journal; The Winnipeg Free Press.**